THE SOVIET ECONOMY:

Myth and Reality

MARSHALL I. GOLDMAN

A SPECTRUM BOOK

PRENTICE-HALL, INC.
Englewood Cliffs, N. J.

Copyright © 1968 by PRENTICE-HALL, INC.
Englewood Cliffs, N. J.

Library of Congress Catalog Card Number: 68-14467

PRINTED IN THE UNITED STATES OF AMERICA

Current printing (last digit):
10   9   8   7   6   5   4   3   2

MARSHALL I. GOLDMAN, *the author of this volume, is Associate Professor of Economics, Wellesley College, and an Associate at Harvard University's Russian Research Center. He is a frequent visitor to the Soviet Union, and has also travelled in Africa and Asia, for first-hand research on Soviet economics and foreign aid programs. He is also the author of* Soviet Marketing, Distribution in a Controlled Economy, Soviet Foreign Aid, *and is the editor of* Comparative Economic Systems: A Reader, *and* Controlling Pollution: The Economics of a Cleaner America *(Prentice-Hall, Inc., 1967). Dr. Goldman has written over fifty articles in scholarly journals throughout the world.*

THE
SOVIET
ECONOMY:

Myth
and
Reality

TO MY PARENTS

PREFACE

As faulty as they may be, our misconceptions about the American economy are minute when compared to our misinformation about the Soviet economy. Just as Delbert A. Snider attempted to improve our understanding of American economic realities in his *Economic Myth and Reality,* so this is an attempt to increase our knowledge of Soviet economic realities.

The task of establishing what is and what is not economic reality in the USSR is not an easy assignment. Not only is it necessary to explain the somehow mystifying mechanics of a national economic system, but it is also necessary to wade through the emotionalism of the cold war and the secretiveness of the Soviets about much of their activity. Fortunately both the cold war and Soviet secrecy no longer cause as much difficulty as they once did. This is partially due to the fact that as economic literacy in the United States increases, it becomes easier to understand economic systems other than our own. We develop an economic perspective that allows us to view the functioning of economic systems regardless of their political coloration. Moreover, the Soviet Union is seeking to become more of a participant in Western economic life. In the process, the cold war has become less of an issue. Thus the Soviets have become less suspicious and secretive, and more generous with their economic information.

With emotions somewhat more relaxed and information more readily available and easily understood, this may be an appropriate juncture to try to balance some of the myths about the Soviet system with some of the realities. The timing seems especially appropriate now that the USSR has celebrated its fiftieth anniversary. In addition to sentiment and thoughts of what might have been, such occasions also evoke reflection on what has gone before and predictions about what lies ahead.

Before beginning, it is necessary to issue a word of caution to the reader. In the 1950's, such disclaimers always began by saying that the writer was not a communist even though he was writing about the USSR. But in the 1930's and again in the 1960's, authors seemed to find it necessary to assure their readers that they were not anti-Marxists. Hopefully the reader will need neither disclaimer as he proceeds through this study. Surely there must be a middle road. Such a course is not always an easy one to follow because of the exaggerations which have been allowed to flourish on both sides. Nonetheless, an effort to distinguish between myth and reality in the USSR demands that no new myths be created or perpetuated in the process of unmasking old misconceptions. How well the writer succeeds in his effort to steer a middle course is left to the reader to judge.

My appreciation is due Diane Hallen, Nancy Braymer, and Rose Di Benedetto for their help in the preparation of this manuscript. Acknowledgment is also due to *Current History* for their permission to reprint portions of my article "Soviet Economic Growth since the Revolution," from their October, 1967, issue (© 1967 by *Current History*) and to *Technology Review* of the Massachusetts Institute of Technology for permission to reprint segments of my article, "What Makes the Soviet Manager Run?" from their July, 1967, issue.

CONTENTS

INTRODUCTION: *What We Know about the Soviet Union and Where We Obtain Our Sources of Information*   1

PART I   Economic Development and the Role of Marxism in the USSR

1   MYTH: *Until the Revolution, Russia was a backward country.*   9

2   MYTH: *The Russian Revolution was the world's first successful Marxist Revolution.*   14

3   MYTH: *Upon coming to power, the Bolsheviks adopted a Marxist blueprint for action which they have been following ever since.*   19

4   MYTH: *Russia needed the Bolshevik Revolution to spark the economic growth necessary to make it the world's second largest industrial power.*   30

PART II   Economic Freedom and
Totalitarianism in the
Soviet Union

5   MYTH: *The Soviet economic system is totalitarian
and by nature it is a slave state.*   39

6   MYTH: *The Soviet Union is a land of milk and
honey where communism has brought
fulfillment and tranquility to everyone.*   62

PART III   Operation of the Economy

7   MYTH: *The Soviet economic system is inefficient
and irrational. There is little sophistication
or innovation.*   79

8   MYTH: *The Soviet economic system is an agile
giant that is outclassing and surpassing all
known economic systems. Because the
state owns all the tools of production, the
Soviet Union is able to avoid wasteful
competition among private manufacturers.
As a result, innovation and flexibility are
encouraged and the Soviet Union leads
the world in industrial technology and
sophistication.*   86

PART IV   The Role of Ideology in
Day-to-Day Economic
Operations

9   MYTH: *Marxism is a vital force in the day-to-day
conduct of economic activity in the Soviet*

Union. All the old capitalistic forms have been tossed into the trash basket of history. 111

10 MYTH: *The Soviet Union is becoming capitalist, and, in a few years, there will be no differences between the Soviet and American economic systems.* 137

PART V Foreign Economic Activity

11 MYTH: *In contrast to the Western world, the Russians have never used foreign trade as an imperialist device to take advantage of other countries.* 145

12 MYTH: *When it comes to foreign trade it is impossible to compete on equal terms with the Russians. Because all foreign trade activities are monopolized in the hands of the state, it is impossible for private traders in a foreign country to command the resources and coordinate themselves as well as a state Ministry of Foreign Trade.* 150

13 MYTH: *The Soviet Union has been a true friend and supporter of the less-developed countries of the world. In both trade and aid, the Russians have neither tied strings nor taken advantage of poorer countries.* 156

CONCLUSION 165

SELECTED BIBLIOGRAPHY 167

INDEX 171

THE SOVIET ECONOMY:

Myth and Reality

INTRODUCTION

What We Know
About the Soviet Union
and Where We Obtain
Our Sources of Information

For those who take the time to learn the Russian language and avail themselves of the vast quantity of material published in the USSR, the Soviet Union is not the supersecret society that many Americans once considered it to be. At the same time, however, it certainly is not an open society, and there are major gaps in the amount of data that is made available. Even the economists (and they are considerably better off than the political scientists when it comes to having access to information), have a difficult time in finding all the facts they need. But the point to stress is that each year, since 1956, the Russians have been making available more and more economic information.

The increase in economic information is not a new departure for the Russians. Actually in the late 1920s and early 1930s, the Russians published immense quantities of data about every possible subject. Their yearly plans contained the most minute detail. It was only in the mid-1930s that Stalin's paranoia and xenophobia led to the suppression of economic data. The fear of capitalist encirclement, Nazi invasion, and the cold war caused him to withhold anything that

1

might possibly provide economic intelligence to the enemy. (And to Stalin, the enemy was the rest of the world.) Even the publication of data on shoe output was no longer permitted. At best, persevering scholars in the West considered themselves fortunate when they uncovered such gems as the percentage increase in steel production or the percentage increase in retail sales from one year to the next. Then, if they were exceptionally clever, they could tie a string of such percentage changes to some prewar figure expressed in tons or rubles. Upon such fragile economic evidence depended our economic assessments of Soviet economic strength.[1]

With the publication of the first postwar statistical handbook in 1956, a generation of economic detectives suddenly found that the other more traditional skills of economic analysis were essential as well. With Stalin dead, the excessive fear and suspicion diminished. There were still significant *lacunae,* but absolute figures reappeared in easy to locate lists. Gradually the amount of published information increased until the size of the yearly statistical handbook has grown to 800 pages. It now contains data such as the average annual wage, a price index, steel production, grain harvests, and national income. Naturally Russian statisticians have not solved the problems of absolute statistical precision any more than their American counterparts have, and there are still statistical shortcomings, but the amount of statistical coverage in the USSR since 1955 has widened beyond reasonable expectation.

The reasons for this change in policy tell us something about the problems common to all industrialized societies. First, as the Soviet economy grew in size, more information about more activities came into being. The problem of keeping all this information secret became too difficult. Not only were foreigners kept in the dark about the country's economy, so were many Russians. Unfortunately this included some Russians whose job it was to evaluate and determine various economic activities. Because most of their information came from the same censored books and periodicals that were sent abroad, they frequently found that they lacked the information necessary to make informed decisions. It was like judging an art show with only half the lights on and the shades down. So from economists, engi-

---

[1] Today, specialists on the Chinese economy confront the same problems.

neers, and even planners came pleas for the release of more information. Finally, as the economy continued to expand, there was less weakness to hide and more prowess to boast about. This, too, necessitated the release of more information.

With the improved flow of statistical data came the publication both here and in the USSR of articles and monographs with increasingly rigorous standards of scholarship. This broadened our knowledge of the Soviet economy even more. There is much more we would like to know, but the improvement has been impressive.

Despite the increase in information, however, it should not be assumed that raw Soviet data can be used without caution. Although Russian statistics usually do measure what they say they measure, it is not always clear what *it is* they say they measure. Thus, in the mid-1930s, Soviet statistics suddenly indicated that the Russian grain harvest had improved considerably more than might have been assumed by reports from the field. The Russian statistics were accurate, it was just that they were not consistent. Without bothering to make much fuss about it, the Russians stopped publishing barn yield figures (grain after it is in the barn) and, instead, suddenly started issuing biological yields (estimates of the harvest in the field). However, there has traditionally been considerable shrinkage between what leaves the field and what enters the barn door. Considering the discontent of the peasants and the widespread pilferage that added to the normal amount of waste that took place, estimates of a 20 per cent difference between the two measurements seem to be conservative. It was not that the harvest figures were actually dishonest; they were just deceptive. To many economists the effect was the same. Several of them accepted the implication that the harvest had increased. To the statistical purist, however, the difference between dishonesty and deception was a crucial one. As opposed to dishonesty, deception means that if only the proper context can be ascertained, the figures can still be used.

Not all the statistical problems can be explained so simply. In some cases, even if everything was as it purported to be, there would still be trouble. This is because there are certain built-in statistical pitfalls that arise from any effort to measure change in an economy, like Russia's, that is undergoing such a radical transformation. One set of hazards stems from the attempt to measure major economic changes. The more dynamic the growth, the harder it is to specify exactly what took place. This is due to the nature of economic change itself and the tools we use to measure it.

In gauging the amount of economic growth that has taken place, the usual procedure is to compare the increase in production of all items from one period to another. The total production effort is measured by multiplying the various goods produced by their prices. This gives us the total value of production in any one year. The next step is to compare the total value of production in one year with that of another year. But if prices should increase from the first year to the second, we would have an exaggerated result. Therefore, to eliminate the distortion of any price changes, it is necessary to use a single year's prices as a guide. In effect, the goods produced in both years are weighted, or multiplied by the prices which were recorded in only one of the years. This eliminates the effect of inflation or deflation, but it creates several new problems. One of these problems is that the process of industrialization generates a fall in the prices of highly fabricated goods such as automobiles and vacuum cleaners. In contrast, the prices of less fabricated goods such as horse carriages and brooms remain constant or increase. Industrialization means mass production, and those goods which suddenly can be produced on the assembly line will be cheaper than they were before. Therefore, if prices of a recent period are used, the role of automobiles and refrigerators will be understated because their prices are usually lower than they were before. In contrast, the role of automobiles and refrigerators will be overstated if prices of an earlier period are used because production earlier in time involved more expensive production techniques.

Until the mid-1950s, the Russians always used the early-year prices which tended to exaggerate the size of their growth. In contrast, American growth was generally expressed in prices of a later period. This understated American growth. Technically, both calculations were correct, but the mechanics of statistical calculation made it inevitable that the USSR would always look as if it were growing even faster than it was in comparison to the United States.

There were other problems that arose because of the peculiarities of the Russian pricing system. For reasons that we shall see, until recently the Russians made no provision for various factors of pro-

4

duction, particularly capital or land costs. Inevitably this meant that relative prices of various goods and services were likely to be poor measures of their economic worth. As a consequence, relative cost and productivity calculations did not always reveal anything that was meaningful. In fact, occasionally such calculations would sometimes indicate just the reverse of what they would have if only there had been a proper accounting of all the factors of production. For example, ignoring the full cost of capital made it inevitable that the planners would favor hydroelectric power plants which used large quantities of capital instead of thermal power plants which used less capital. This was natural since the day to day cost of coal in thermal power was more expensive than the day to day cost of water running over the dam. Unless some recognition was taken of the large quantity of scarce capital used in building the dam, hydroelectric power would always appear cheaper. There were similar problems in trying to determine what goods to export and import. On occasion such studies would indicate that the Russians should import what they had actually been exporting, and vice versa.

Because of such difficulties, a few of which continue to the present time, some Russians feel that Western calculations of Russian economic activity are actually superior to similar calculations made within the USSR itself. Thus, A. G. Aganbegian, the Director of the Novosibirsk Institute of Economics, was reliably reported to have declared to Soviet economists that "it is easier for us to obtain much statistical data from American magazines than from the Central Statistical Agency in the USSR. . . ." [2] As flattering and at the same time as unsettling as such a statement is, it does suggest that American efforts to interpret Soviet statistics are careful enough to warrant a strong measure of confidence. It is this research which will be utilized in the present study.

[2] *Bandiera Rossa,* Rome, July, 1965, p. 6, as quoted by *The ASTE Bulletin,* Summer, 1965, p. 4.

PART I

Economic
Development
and the Role
of Marxism
in the USSR

MYTH: *Until the Revolution, Russia was a backward country.*

In the mythology that has evolved to romanticize the admittedly impressive growth of the Soviet economy, prerevolutionary Russia is often depicted as an economic pygmy. The argument is sometimes extended to imply that since Russia in 1914 was in about the same economic straits as China, India, and Egypt in 1960, the developing countries should pattern their strategy of economic development after the actions of the USSR. Only in this way, so the argument goes, can they industrialize in an equally short period of time.

Such statements are more wishful thinking than accurate history. It is true that Russia before World War I was economically inferior to England, Germany, and France, not to mention the United States. Even France produced more than double what Russia manufactured in 1913, and the figures were considerably higher for comparisons with Germany and England. But it is too much to say that Russia's economy was as backward as those of most of the countries in Asia and Africa today. Because of the statistical uncertainties involved, it is impossible to make an unreserved statement, but Russia in 1913 may have been economically superior to Japan and perhaps Italy. All three countries were early examples of what is today called a *dual economy:* A very modern sector existed simultaneously with a very primitive sector in both industry and agriculture. But in absolute gross national product (GNP) and possibly even in per capita GNP, Russia was the more developed country.

9

According to both Russian and Western sources, Russian growth between the early 1880s and 1913 was very impressive.[1] It was in this brief 23-year period that Russia emerged from the ranks of the economically impoverished. By 1913, steel production was five times larger than it was in 1890. There was almost a tenfold increase in the mining of coal.[2] The railroad network almost tripled in size.[3] Especially notable was the building of the Trans-Siberian Railroad, one of the most impressive engineering accomplishments of the time. Comparable expansion in other industrial sectors resulted in an average annual rate of industrial growth of about 8 per cent in the 1890s. According to Alexander Gerschenkron, the rate of growth reached an even higher level by the end of the decade. The growth of the 1890s, however, was followed by a depression in 1900. Nonetheless, the five slow years that followed were compensated for by a renewed spurt of growth. From 1905 to 1914, the average rate of industrial growth again rose, this time to about 6 per cent per year.[4]

The whoosh of economic growth brought the Soviet economy a long way in a short time. For anyone with statistical compulsiveness, such comparisons are always less than satisfying, but there are indications that the use of mechanized power per worker in "large-scale" Russian industry was higher than it was in Germany and France.[5] Of course this was a very unbalanced type of growth. As we have come to expect in a dual economy, some industries simply did not develop and many areas of the country were completely unaffected by the changes made elsewhere. But, whatever the unevenness, a major transformation had been wrought in the industrial sector.

After an even longer period of stagnation, the agricultural sector began to show signs of growth. Despite the emancipation of the peasants in 1861, not much real change occurred in agriculture for several decades. Most peasants found themselves tied to their villages and unable to leave the communal associations which gained new

[1] Alexander Gerschenkron, *Economic Backwardness in Historical Perspective*. Cambridge, Mass.: Harvard University Press, 1962, p. 219; also, Peter I. Lyashchenko, *History of the National Economy of Russia*. New York: The Macmillan Company, 1949, pp. 525, 669.

[2] Lyashchenko, *op. cit.*, pp. 528-29, 688-89.

[3] *Ibid.*, p. 502.

[4] Gerschenkron, *op. cit.*, p. 133.

[5] Lyashchenko, *op. cit.*, p. 673.

power in the wake of the emancipation. Two factors helped to pave the way for a significant improvement in rural conditions. Responding to considerable unrest in the countryside, the Czarist government finally decided to lighten the burden of the peasant and free him from the remaining obligations of his emancipation. In 1906, Stolypin, then the Minister of the Interior, pushed through new legislation which he hoped would stimulate production and accumulation by the peasants. Under the new law, the peasants were encouraged to set up their own farms and move out of the traditional farming commune. Steps were also taken to free the peasant from the financial burdens incurred at the time of emancipation. To obtain the political stability and economic growth in the countryside that he was seeking, Stolypin resolved to "wager not on the needy and the drunken but on the strong—the sturdy individual proprietor." In this way he hoped to provide higher profits for the more able peasants. They in turn would be stimulated to increase their harvests which would make for a more productive and prosperous country.

In addition to encouraging production, the government also facilitated the marketing of what was harvested. It subsidized the construction of the nationwide railroad network mentioned on the previous page. This made it possible to move the harvest from interior points that had previously been inaccessible. Together, the impact of improved transportation and effective incentives led to a significant growth in agricultural production in the years just before the war.

Supplementing the growth in industry and agriculture, progress was also being made in the fields of education and science. The official census of 1897, the only one taken in prerevolutionary Russia, indicated that only 21 per cent of the population was literate. Yet there was growing recognition of the need for education, and laws were passed in 1908 calling for the compulsory and free education of all children from the ages of 8 to 11. Moreover, some areas of scientific work in Russia were quite sophisticated even by world standards. In fact, with scientists and scholars like M. V. Lomanosov, the physicist and historian, N. I. Lobachevsky, the mathematician, D. I. Mendeleev, the chemist, I. P. Pavlov, the physiologist, and K. E. Tsiolkovsky, the pioneer of rocketry, it seemed that Russia had greater strength at the top of the educational ladder than at the bottom. Naturally, until education was open to the masses, the climb of scholars and managers to the top of the educational pyramid would be limited and not reflect the country's full potential. Yet, by 1917, almost 25,000 patents had been issued to Russian inventors. Although many of these were applied only outside of Russia and even though this was only one-tenth the number of patents issued in Germany, it was still something more than the performance we think of when we use the term *backward country*. Moreover, prerevolutionary Russia did give birth to such literary giants as Pushkin, Gogol, Tolstoy, and Dostoevsky, and to musical geniuses like Moussorgsky and Tchaikovsky. The present-day USSR has yet to produce a comparable list. Certainly there was much that remained to be done before educational opportunity and scientific research would permeate all of Russia, but a start had been made.

The effect of all these important developments is often overlooked. But the Russian economic bear had begun to stir. Unfortunately, history will never know what would have happened if World War I and the Bolshevik Revolution had not interrupted the progress.

Those in the developing countries who look to the Soviet Union as a model for themselves often are unaware of just how much progress had been made. In comparison to Russia of 1913, the countries of Africa and Asia are at a much lower economic level. If nothing else, the Russian population prior to World War I was about one-fourth the population in present-day India and one-fifth that of China. Consequently, on a per capita basis, Chinese and Indian production levels in 1950 and even in 1957 and 1960 were considerably below Russia's in 1913. In some cases, Russian production was greater even on an absolute basis. Considering that world levels of production were considerably lower in the early 1900s and that therefore the distance between the leaders and the laggards was a good deal shorter, it should be evident that Russia's relative as well as its absolute situation was much better than that of China and India.

All arguments which try to show that the preconditions for economic development were not as hopeless as many have come to believe do not necessarily mean that the Czarist government was a good or benevolent regime. Some of the abuses committed in the name of official government policy were as bad as anything our more modern totalitarian or autocratic governments have been able to devise. It would take considerable effort to show that the Czarist government was worth preserving. However, the fact remains that some improve-

12

ments were being made, and the future appeared to offer considerably more hope than the past.

REALITY: *Russia under the Czars was underdeveloped, but there were signs of progress. Moreover, prerevolutionary Russia's position in relation to the developed countries of Europe was considerably better than the relation of such countries as India and China to the developed world of the 1950s and 1960s.*

CHAPTER 2

MYTH: *The Russian Revolution was the world's first successful Marxist Revolution.*

Although they continued to be shocking, by the end of the nineteenth century, revolutions were not especially new. The American and the French Revolutions of the eighteenth century had been copied throughout Latin America with varying degrees of success. Moreover, it was sometimes hard to distinguish between civil and revolutionary wars, especially when they were unsuccessful. The formation of the Paris Commune in 1870 appeared to be a revolution with a Marxist orientation, but it was soon put down. In Germany, there had been no revolution, but the Social Democratic Party appeared menacingly ready to take over the government. As the world's largest Marxist party, it preached revolution but gradually came to practice a more pragmatic and accommodating policy. As its bureaucratic hierarchy grew in size and ponderousness, its revolutionary fervor diminished.

Thus by the start of World War I, after much agitation and a schism of both anarchists and revisionists, the chances of an all-out Marxist revolution were greater in theory than in practice. Consequently it was with a sense of surprise to say the least that the world heard Lenin's announcement that his Communist Party had successfully conducted a revolution and seized power.

But was this a Marxist Revolution? Admittedly it is hard to say precisely what a Marxist Revolution is supposed to be. Moreover it is difficult to make any rigid classification about what is and is not

Marxist. In the course of his life, Marx kept changing his mind about what he did and did not want. Therefore it is possible to find a little something in Marx for everyone even if it is contradictory. As the economist *Pareto* once said, the statements of Karl Marx are like bats. From one angle they resemble birds, while from another view they look like mice. Thus one can see what one wants to see in Marx, uninhibited by what really might be there.

Using such leeway, Marx's followers set off on all kinds of tangents. This should have been expected because by their nature revolutionaries usually oppose authority; inevitably they tend to substitute their own rules, which in turn appear as imposed authority to younger revolutionaries. Like it or not, even revolutionaries seem to have thirtieth birthdays and some grow even older. After a few years of this factionalism, Marx himself had become so perplexed by the bickering and reinterpretation that he was reported to have declared that he was not a Marxist. Nonetheless, as loose as Marxist doctrine is, even a true believer in 1917 would have had to believe extra hard before he could convince himself that Russia was the time and the place for a Marxist revolution. That many true believers did manage to convince themselves speaks more for the power of faith than for logical consistency.

The hardest argument to overcome was that only in his later life did Marx ever dream that a revolution would take place first in a country like Russia. Marx always assumed it would occur in a country like Germany, England, the Netherlands or France. After all, if this was to be a proletarian revolution, it was necessary to have an industrial working class that was not only large in absolute numbers but was large relative to the rest of the population. We have just finished trying to show that Russia was not the most backward country, but in our enthusiasm, I hope we did not go so far as to imply that it was one of the most advanced countries. Russia in 1913 and after the war had only a small urban working force in relation to the total population. More than 80 per cent of the population at the time lived in rural areas. According to official Soviet figures, only 17 per cent of the population was classified as workers and white collar employees.[1] It takes considerable stretching to argue that such a small percentage

[1] *Dostizheniia Sovetskoi Vlasti Za 40 Let V Tsifrakh.* Moscow, Tsentralnoe Statisticheskoi Upravlenie, 1957, p. 11.

of the population would be able to lead the rest of the population into revolution. After all, the Communist Party was to be the vanguard of the proletariat, but if the revolution was to be successful, the proletariat had to be numerous enough to lead.

Because he recognized the absurdity of his position, Lenin broadened his revolutionary base as much as possible. In the Russian context, this meant that he would have to include the peasantry. As a tactic, this was perfectly reasonable; however, as Marxism, this was virtually heretical because Marx always argued that it was the proletariat who would lead the revolution. The peasants were usually thought to be too conservative, almost like the bourgeoisie.

As in any political battle, if the peasants were to offer their support, they had to be given something in return. The only thing Lenin's proletariat had to give them was the landlord's land. This explains the inclusion of "land" in Lenin's revolutionary battle cry "Bread, Land, and Peace." The slogan attracted the hungry and the war weary and it also whetted the appetite of the peasants who had only begun to sense the advantages of private ownership under the Stolypin Reforms. But, while it won Lenin political support, it created an ideological headache. By turning over land to the peasants, Lenin found himself furthering the acquisitive instincts of one of the most conservative of all economic classes. Peasants traditionally have been regarded as one of the most reactionary forces in society. Later, Lenin and his successors were to find that their compromise with the peasants would come back to plague them.

There were some who argued that the absence of a large proletariat class and an alliance with the peasants did not matter. Implicitly they agreed that a Marxist revolution in Russia in 1917 was a contradiction in terms. A true revolution could only come in Western Europe. Previously, however, whenever it looked as if West European revolutionaries had a good revolution in prospect, Russia, the "gendarme of Europe," would always step in and put a stop to it. This happened in 1830 and 1863 in Poland and in 1848 in Hungary. Therefore for a revolution to succeed in Europe, it was necessary to immunize the Russians. One way to do this would be to install a revolutionary government in St. Petersburg, as Leningrad, then the capital of Russia used to be called. Based on this reasoning, it did not matter how impure ideologically the revolutionary government was in Russia. It was only to be a holding operation until their proletarian comrades in the more advanced countries of Europe could throw off their oppressive yokes.

We know by now that even with the immobilization of the gendarme of Europe, the advanced countries like Germany, Holland, England, and France never did join the ranks with their own revolutions. (There were some who tried to make revolution in these countries, but with no success.) Strictly speaking, at this point a good Marxist would have said that the whole Russian revolution was a mistake. As some in fact did argue, the best thing to have done would have been to retreat a step and set up a bourgeoisie government. As they correctly surmised, the imposition of a proletarian revolution and a dictatorship of the proletariat before a country is ready for it will lead to all sorts of abuses on the part of a state bureaucracy. Marx intended that the oppression that comes with industrialization should be generated and directed by the bourgeoisie, not the state. Thus it would be the bourgeoisie and not the state that would be cast in the role as the oppressor. After all, the capitalists were very able, and, if they were left alone long enough, they would build a productive economic structure. Upon the completion of that structure, the bourgeoisie could then be dispensed with and the society would be taken over by a much more benevolent bureaucracy under the supervision of the proletariat and the Communist Party. However, if the bureaucracy was forced to act prematurely and create the industrial structure itself with the accompanying pressures and problems, then the state would be regarded as the oppressor, not the bourgeoisie. Furthermore there would be no means available to check the abuses and power of the bureaucracy after the more draconic measures had been taken.

But the majority of Lenin's supporters were not such ideological purists. They were content to let the ideology fit the time. Once it was clear that the proletariat of Western Europe were not able or willing to follow, then the Bolsheviks decided to accept the theory of permanent revolution. This was the idea that a revolution could come to one country which would then maintain its revolutionary identity although surrounded by hostile imperialists.

Subsequently other communist regimes in other countries found it necessary to rely on the same coalition of workers and peasants that had been necessary in the Soviet Union. This became inevitable, as

17

the revolutionary movement seemed to find its greatest support in agrarian countries. Only when Soviet troops were nearby to assist in the generation of revolutionary fervor were there any exceptions to this general rule. As the percentage of proletariat in the population grew smaller, the more the revolutionary movement came to rely on the peasant class. This accommodation and dilution of pure ideology to meet the needs of local practice resembled what often happens to a religion as it spreads through different cultures. A Catholic in Italy finds the service of a Catholic in Ireland to be different from his own. Both of them would find the service of a Catholic in Latin America or in Africa to be even more distinct. The spread of Marxism experienced the same adulteration. In the extreme case of China, Mao Tse-tung has come to base his revolutionary drive almost exclusively on the peasants and the countryside. Without doubt, this has proven to be good revolutionary strategy, but it does not really have much to do with what Marx was talking about. As might be expected, this has not affected the success of any revolutions, but if Marx were alive today, he certainly would be hard pressed to explain how what passes today as a communist revolution is related to his original program.

REALITY: *Marxism may have appealed to the Russian revolutionaries as an ideology for revolution, but Marxism was not intended for predominantly agricultural countries. As a result, the character of communist ideology and communist government had to be altered to fit local circumstances and needs so that in the extreme case, it has become more the revolutionary doctrine of and for the peasants than the proletariat.*

CHAPTER 3

MYTH: *Upon coming to power, the Bolsheviks adopted a Marxist blueprint for action which they have been following ever since.*

If it is difficult to determine in which countries Marx said the revolution would take place, it is even more difficult to decide what Marx expected would happen once the revolution had occurred. The confusion multiplies when the revolution erupts in a country other than one of those selected by Marx.

The reason for all this uncertainty is that Marx seldom concerned himself with the operations and problems of a communist society. He was primarily a student of capitalism. Consequently his main concern was the revolution and the disintegration of an economic system, not its construction and expansion. Only rarely did Marx make any comments about what the new communist society would be like. Perhaps the best example of such a study is *The Critique of the Gotha Program,* and even that is only a rough sketch.

With such an incomplete blueprint, it is sometimes hard to argue that a particular action would or would not have fit into Marx's scheme. Yet clearly there are some economic activities he presumably would have opposed, even if they were explained away as being only a temporary expedient. As we shall see, temporary expedients have a way of becoming permanent encumbrances, especially when the Marxist revolution takes place in a country which is not among the economically advanced. Then the state becomes responsible for building up the industrial framework which theoretically should already have been completed. As we have seen, this usually forces the state to assume the role of a forceful accumulator, a role which it never seems to want to give up. Inevitably democratic rights are sacrificed in the process and only slowly if ever regained.

In Chapter 9 we shall consider whether various economic practices of the USSR would qualify for the Marxist seal of approval. In this section, we shall restrict ourselves to the broad structural developments and see if the Russian Communists acted according to Marxist precepts in the early years of their power.

One of the first actions after the revolution was the expropriation of private property. Seemingly this was in line with Marxist ideology. However, Marxism had little to do with what happened. For the most part confiscation tended to take place almost spontaneously. Returning home from the battlefront, the peasants simply threw out the landlords and took over the acreage they had previously rented. But this amounted to no more than substitution of one form of ownership for another. The peasants instead of the landlords became the owners. This often meant the new owner was just as conservative as his predecessor.

Ideology was similarly upended in industry. Prior to the revolution, Lenin called for complete nationalization, but immediately after the revolution most of the communist leaders changed their minds and called for moderation and patience. In the reaction and civil war that ensued, there was widespread chaos. The communists wanted all the production and stability they could find. Therefore they opposed confiscation because they feared it would lead to further disruption of the economy. Furthermore, they recognized that some of the old managers would support the new government if the transition to state control was not violent. Actually, the old managers were needed to run the factories. There was a shortage of skilled managers who were also communists. Not many members of the proletarian class had training enough to take over the managerial function.

Pleas for moderation however were of little or no avail. To some extent the factory workers were caught up in the same emotional tide as the peasants. They, too, wanted to throw out the old owners. Unfortunately, there was a big difference between taking over a farm which was much more of a self-contained unit and a factory which depended on other sources for its raw materials as well as its customers. If nothing else, the peasant could always consume his produce himself. But the factory had to sell to and buy from others. Accordingly, when some workers took over their factories and tried to set themselves up as self-contained units, they ran into immediate problems. It was ridiculous to expect that the rest of the world would unconditionally meet the terms called for by the new factory committees. Increasingly the Soviet leaders began to realize that the workers were reacting in a syndicalist fashion. Their attitudes verged on anarchy. The workers were urging that each factory should be a castle unto itself. This was hardly a course that could be maintained in a society which was attempting to complete the process of industrialization.

For a time Lenin tried to fight these syndicalist tendencies, and decrees were issued in February, 1918, prohibiting the confiscation of factories without specific permission from the ruling authorities in Moscow.[1] Ultimately, Lenin decided he could not hold back the tide. Therefore he decided to roll with it and thereby attempt to guide and control it. Still it was not until June 28, 1918, that a decree was finally adopted ordering the nationalization of all large-scale industry. It was like turning off the lights after the power has gone off. Only in retrospect could it possibly have been argued that confiscation of property was in accord with Marxist precepts. Even then, such rationalization amounted to nothing more than trying to make the best out of a bad situation.

Following the period from 1917 to 1921, which was subsequently called *War Communism,* the Communists made a major shift in policy. By 1921, Lenin had managed to eliminate most of the opposition of the more conservative segments of society. However, he encountered a new form of opposition. Lenin suddenly found that many of his early supporters such as the poorer peasants and even the sailors at the Kronstadt Naval Base outside of Leningrad were beginning to protest the policies of his government in agriculture and its inability to provide enough food in the cities. This hurt because these same sailors had been the source of Lenin's main support during

[1] Maurice Dobb, *Soviet Economic Development Since 1917.* London: Routledge and Kegan Paul, Ltd., 1966, p. 90.

the November attack on the Czar's Winter Palace in Leningrad. When allies like the militant Kronstadt sailors defected, it was clear to Lenin that he must be doing something wrong.

Recognizing that some radical changes were necessary, Lenin proclaimed a New Economic Policy (NEP) for the country in March, 1921. He decided that it would be necessary to take one step backward in order to make what he promised would be two steps forward. But the steps were so far backward that some critics were convinced that Lenin had stepped back into capitalism.

To bring some order out of the economic chaos that existed, Lenin realized that one of the first things he would have to do would be to restore the flow of consumer goods, including nonfood products. Food was in short supply in the urban areas, and what few products were produced in the urban factories somehow never found their way to the peasants. Finding there was nothing they could exchange for their food, the peasants had simply cut down on the amount of food they offered to exchange. When Lenin sent out troops to confiscate the food, the peasants decided to resist even more.

Because he felt that further pressure by the state and further monopolization of trade through state-controlled stores would do nothing to alleviate this situation, Lenin decided to reverse himself. First, he decreed that henceforth peasants would only have a fixed quota of food to deliver. Everything above that could be sold freely at higher prices. Like a progressive piece rate in its impact, the more the peasant produced, the higher the price he was paid for that extra output. This was meant to stimulate the peasants to extra effort, and in a very short period of time it did. Second, he decided to permit the reappearance of private traders. In this way he hoped that profit-seeking merchants would dig out hidden stocks of goods and encourage the production of new ones. Together this would lead to a rebirth of commerce and retail sales. Lenin was right. Private merchants opened up small shops in the cities and peddlers, called *Nepmen,* spread through the countryside selling factory-made products for food.

Throughout the whole NEP period, the state maintained control over what Lenin called "the commanding heights." [2] Thus heavy industry and the banks were retained under state ownership to ensure

---

[2] Maurice Dobb, *op. cit.,* p. 145.

that there could be no major subversion of communist control. Nonetheless, private ownership in the fringe areas of the economy was encouraged to get the economy moving again. As we have seen, this policy was highly successful. By 1928, recovery from the damage of the civil war and revolution had been completed. Still, no matter how Lenin's steps are rationalized, certainly the NEP period cannot be considered part of any Marxist blueprint. If anything, it was recognition that Russia was not ready for any jump into complete state ownership, a step which presumably a Marxist state would have had to take.

Lenin died in the course of the New Economic Policy, and Stalin assumed control. No one knows what course Lenin would have taken had he lived, but his moderation in the NEP period suggests his subsequent policies might have been more temperate than Stalin's. Certainly it is hard to see how they could have been any more intemperate.

With reconstruction completed, Stalin addressed himself to the problem of the Soviet Union's future. He and his advisers were worried that growth in the future would not be as easy. Economic growth in a period of reconstruction is usually quite rapid. In some cases, all that is needed to set an idle factory in motion is to find a new source of raw materials. In other cases, more extensive repairs may have to be made. For the most part, however, there is no need to make extensive capital investments. Therefore the capital–output ratio is very low, which means a little capital investment in the form of inventory and repairs will generate an impressive rate of growth. But with reconstruction completed, it was anticipated that the capital–output ratio would increase and more capital would be required to produce the same increase in industrial output. Along with several economists of the time, Stalin began to wonder whether or not the Soviet Union would be able to generate the much larger quantities of capital he now thought would be necessary to build brand new projects. If not, then the growth rate would fall. In the debate that was generated over this problem, apparently there was little mention of the fact that Russia had managed rapid growth with new projects (albeit with some help from foreign investments) in the 1890s and from 1905 to 1913 (see Chapter 1).

Stalin had other problems as well. Because of the concessions that were made to win peasant support for the Revolution, the state found

23

that it was not enough to issue a decree that the harvest be a certain tonnage of grain. As long as the peasants were in possession of their own little farms, they could not be relied upon to supply a steady flow of grain to market. Even later, when the state assumed ownership of the farms, Stalin found that decrees to the peasants had little impact. It was easy for the peasant to cut himself off from the market. By planting just enough for his own family, he could be assured of an adequate food supply and some homemade clothes. He could do without almost everything else, except salt. The peasant had displayed this kind of independence during the period of War Communism, when many of them refused to market any of their produce. The NEP reforms were meant to change this. As the peasants began to respond to the improved incentives, their output increased. This, however, had the effect of bringing down the price of food. Simultaneously, after an initial drop, the price of industrial goods rose as factories found their needs mounting rapidly.[3] The rise in the prices of manufactured goods was accelerated by a rapid increase in the flow of currency from the printing press, which led inevitably to inflation. The divergence in industrial and agricultural prices came to be known as the *scissors crisis*. As the peasants saw that the harder they worked, the less they were able to buy, they began to hold back their surpluses again. This jeopardized the flow of food to the cities and to export markets.[4]

With time, as the NEP reforms brought about increased factory production and improved distribution, price levels returned to more balanced levels, but government officials decided that they could not depend on a smooth flow of marketed output from the peasants. Furthermore, the road ahead would probably be particularly bumpy because of a decision by the government about future price policy. After some debate, it was decided to hold down prices on agricultural products. At first, supporters of the peasant had argued that higher prices would stimulate higher outputs and higher marketings. Critics of this position asserted that this would amount to turning over the fruits of the revolution to the peasants, and, after all, the proletariat were expected to enjoy some of the benefits. It was realized that the urban worker would not have been very pleased to find that the price of his food and therefore his cost of living had increased. There

[3] Maurice Dobb, *op. cit.*, p. 162.
[4] *Ibid.*, p. 164.

24

seemed to be little appreciation of the fact that after a time, an increase in farm output would probably have led to a natural fall in prices. Those who did see this were not pacified either since they feared a fall in prices might in itself set off another peasant boycott. All in all, unless something was done to revoke the concessions that had been made to the peasants at the time of the revolution, Stalin felt that the state would forever be at their mercy. So it was that Stalin became displeased with the agricultural situation as it existed in the 1920s. He concluded that something would have to be done to break the hammerlock of the peasants on the future of the rest of the country.

Stalin's need for a final solution to the problem seemed to become especially urgent because of what he interpreted to be a renewal of the peasant boycott in 1926 and 1927. In a significant article, Jerzy F. Karcz of the University of California has found evidence to show that Stalin himself may have been confused about the actions of the peasants in 1926 and 1927.[5] Stalin mixed up two sets of figures. The higher set of figures was used to show how high the marketing of food was in 1913, and the lower set was used to show how conditions had deteriorated in the crop year 1926-1927. It is not clear, says Karcz, whether Stalin himself knew that he was confusing the two concepts. According to the figures Stalin used, *gross marketings* by the peasants of grain in 1913 were 21.3 million tons, or 26 per cent of the harvest. But, in the crop year 1926-1927, Stalin indicated deliveries fell by one-half to 10.3 million tons or 13.3 per cent of the harvest (see Table 1). Karcz shows, however, that these figures were not comparable. It was like comparing onions and cheddar cheese. At best, one ends up with a fancy before-dinner appetizer; at worst, with a case of economic indigestion.

Although agricultural production did fall, Karcz convincingly shows that Stalin should have also used *gross marketings* for the 1926-1927 period if he wanted to be statistically consistent. Instead, for some reason, Stalin used a *net marketing concept*. This was of necessity a lower figure because it was *gross marketings minus* any grain the peasants bought for themselves. After fulfilling their compulsory delivery obligations, the peasants went out and repurchased large

[5] Jerzy F. Karcz, "Thoughts on the Grain Problem," *Soviet Studies,* Apr., 1967, p. 339.

TABLE 1 STALIN'S INCONSISTENT USE OF MARKETING FIGURES

| Output Figures | Marketing Figures | | | | | |
| | Gross | | Net | | Stalin's | |
Gross Output, Millions of Tons	Millions of Tons	Per Cent of Output	Millions of Tons	Per Cent of Output	Millions of Tons	Per Cent of Output
1913 81.9	21.3	26	9.4	11.5	21.3	26
1926-1927 76.8-78.3	16.2	20.7	10.3	13.3	10.3	13.3

Source: Jerzy F. Karcz, "Thoughts on the Grain Problem," *Soviet Studies*, April, 1967, pp. 402, 408.

quantities of the same grain. This seemingly abnormal reaction on their part was due to the fact that the price of grain, as we have seen, was kept low to hold down peasant profits. But with such low prices, the peasants found it profitable to buy back the grain and use it for feed for their livestock which sold at a very high price.

Accordingly, if Stalin had also used a *gross marketing* figure for 1926-1927, he would have been forced to conclude that marketings had not really fallen that much. *Gross marketings* in 1926-1927 were 16.2 million tons or 20.7 per cent. This is a drop from the 26 per cent of 1913, but not as much as everyone had been led to believe. Moreover, the drop in grain production and marketing was more than offset by an increase in the production of higher protein products such as milk and meat. Therefore, the total amount marketed, including grain *and* animal products, actually rose. Similarly, Karcz shows that the fall in grain exports was partially offset by a rise in export of other farm products. Instead of the pessimism and concern that followed from Stalin's incorrect use of marketing figures, there should have been optimism and hope. The switch in production and marketing to high protein foods is usually considered the mark of economic development.

Whatever the reason for Stalin's misuse of statistics, it did create the impression of an impending food crisis. The fear of such a disaster plus his desire to eliminate the stranglehold of the peasants once and for all led Stalin to call for the collectivization of agriculture. Under this policy, Russian peasants were urged and ultimately compelled to form collective farms (*kolkhozy*). To do this, they had to give up their land (except for a small area which they were later allowed to farm privately), almost all their livestock, and any machinery they might have had. Henceforth all farming was to be done collectively with the work and the profits shared jointly.

The reaction of the peasants to this new proposal was one of tremendous hostility and resistance. Millions of lives were lost in what was later called the *Second Russian Revolution*. For centuries the peasants had been serfs and tenants. During all those years they yearned for the ownership of what, after a time, they considered their land. Then suddenly, in the emotional wave of 1917 and 1918, they attained what they had sought for so long. In the years that followed, there were pressures and problems, but the land was theirs. Their conservative yearnings were finally satisfied. Suddenly all of this was taken away. They had been double crossed. The land had been given to them in exchange for their support during the Revolution; then it was nationalized by the state and they had lost it all.

Again the question arises: Did the collectivization of agriculture fit into the Marxist blueprint? Conceivably it could have. Collectivization meant the end of private ownership. But the destruction that ensued was certainly a high price to pay. If anything, there is good reason to believe that economic progress, if not ideological purity, would have been advanced with only slightly more moderate policies. Moreover, the increased production that a slightly higher price for grain would have stimulated would probably not have resulted in a transfer of economic wealth from the urban to the rural sector as Stalin feared. On the contrary, if there had been no collectivization, there would not have been so much suffering and protest. This in turn would have meant increased production on the farm and a better standard of living for the urban residents.

It is not just that Stalin's agricultural policy created a drag on the economy that even now has not been completely remedied; it is also that he acted more out of pragmatism than ideology to eliminate what he thought to be an impending agricultural crisis. In the process, of course, he created his own crisis, but it is hard to see how ideology more than pragmatism was the main guide to his actions.

Marxist ideology seems to have been more of an influence in the industrial sector. Lenin sought complete ownership by the state of private industry. Stalin gradually reduced the amount of private ownership that had been permitted during the New Economic Policy and, in the crop year 1927-1928, announced the inauguration of the first of a series of Five Year Plans. Variations of these plans have continued to the present day, interrupted only by war and by over- and under-fulfillment (see Table 2).

TABLE 2 THE FIVE-YEAR PLANS

10/1928-12/1932	First Five-Year Plan
1933-1937	Second Five-Year Plan
1938-War	Third Five-Year Plan
1945-1950	Fourth Five-Year Plan
1951-1955	Fifth Five-Year Plan
1956-1960	Sixth Five-Year Plan (overexpectations)
1959-1965	Seven-Year Plan
1966-1970	New Five-Year Plan

Today, planning is considered a hallmark of a Marxist society. Lenin took the first hesitant steps in this direction with his GOELRO (State Commission for Electrification) introduced in March, 1920. This group was to draw up a plan for the electrification of the country. In Lenin's words "Communism is the Soviet system (councils or the new forms of government administration) plus the electrification of the entire country." Of course, it took much more than that, but this was a way of focusing attention on the need to promote electrification.

Subsequently, GOELRO was merged into Gosplan (the State Planning Commission) in February, 1921. It was Gosplan which drew up the preliminary work and ultimately the first complete Five-Year Plan for the period October, 1928, to the end of 1932. There is no question but that the utilization of a state planning organization to draw up a nationwide plan was a new and ingenious innovation. Many Russians acknowledge that the concept of a plan derived from the practice of individual American firms that found it necessary to project their budget and production needs far in advance. Leon Smolinski of Boston College has found that in addition, early Russian planning relied heavily on the model proposed by Professor Karl

Ballod of Germany.[6] But whatever the un-Marxist origins of the state plan, and however fragile the data and the degree of control, nothing comparable to this comprehensive planning had ever been attempted before on a nationwide basis, nor had all the industries of a country ever been put under unified state rule.

It could be argued that the switch to planning was Marxist because it put control of the economy in the hands of the state for the first time. At the same time, however, the desire for economic development played as important and probably a more important role than Marxism in the decision to adopt a Five-Year Plan. This should not be interpreted to mean that the plan as a Marxist instrument and the plan as a means for economic development are necessarily mutually exclusive. Clearly the plan could have served both purposes. However, given Stalin's mania for growth, it does seem fair to suggest that he was more concerned about expansion than doctrine.

REALITY: *Even though some of the measures they took could be considered steps in the direction of ideological purity, for the most part the Bolsheviks were motivated primarily by practical considerations. The closest they came to following Marxist precepts was their nationalization of industry in the late 1920s and their adoption of a system of annual and Five-Year Plans. But, on balance, it is hard to deny that the institutional forms adopted by the Russians were dictated as much by the needs of economic development as ideological conformity.*

[6] Leon Smolinski, "Planning Without Theory, 1917-1967," *Survey,* July, 1967, p. 108.

CHAPTER 4

MYTH: *Russia needed the Bolshevik Revolution to spark the economic growth necessary to make it the world's second largest industrial power.*

As the pragmatist once said, it is hard to argue with success. Because the Russians have carried themselves from the rear ranks of the European laggards to the front ranks of the world leaders, they have managed to forestall many arguments. But even if it is conceded that the Russians might have grown at a significantly lower rate of growth if they had adopted some other form of economic organization, it might nonetheless be possible to show that equally rapid rates of growth could also have been achieved in some other way. If we should find that there was no other alternative that could have assured the same success, then indeed it is necessary to acknowledge that some of the political excesses of the Stalinist period might have been needed to produce rapid economic growth. By the same token, however, if it can be demonstrated that equally rapid growth or almost as rapid growth could have been obtained by some other less draconic methods, then it seems fair to conclude that Soviet economic growth may not have been worth the cost of a Stalinist regime.

Under the best of circumstances, such questions require some very heroic assumptions, but they must be made if thoughtful guidance is to be provided other countries which confront the same situation. With the passage of time, there is less and less tendency to ask such questions because history tends to favor the dramatic. Historians concentrate on the greater glory that was Egypt under the Pharaohs, Rome under Caesar, and France under Napolean. The suffering inflicted on the enemy or the out-of-favor is neglected in the rush to admire the monuments that survive. The same thing is beginning to happen within the Soviet Union. There are some who are trying to forget Stalin's excesses. Therefore, to ensure balance in judging history, it is necessary periodically to ask if collectivization, forced-draft industrialization, and Stalin were necessary.

The first point to remember is that, prior to Russia's entrance into World War I, it was experiencing a very rapid rate of growth. Although there were bad as well as good years, we noticed earlier that Alexander Gerschenkron has estimated that the average annual rate of industrial growth in the 1890s was as high as 8 per cent and about 6 per cent between 1905 and 1914. Conceivably, somewhat similar rates could have been maintained after the war without much more strain than had been required earlier. Nonetheless fifteen years later under Stalin it became fashionable to argue that such high rates of growth require large and, it was thought, unavailable capital resources. In contrast, not many in the prerevolutionary period seemed to feel that future rapid growth would require a radical uprooting of the economy and society. Perhaps it was not a problem then because it was assumed there would always be substantial inflows of foreign capital. Yet some authorities like Gerschenkron argue that economic growth in Russia was in fact becoming self-sustaining without the need for large quantities of outside aid. In any case, a small amount of foreign investment, whatever its disadvantages, might have been better than the chaos and suffering which eventually ensued during the collectivization of agriculture in the late 1920s and early 1930s. Perhaps it was for just this reason that Lenin and much later Khrushchev *did* seek outside credits and investments. Stalin refused to do this. The result was death and destruction.

Moreover, not only was prerevolutionary Russia growing at an impressive rate prior to World War I, but there were other countries at the time that seemed to have attained equally striking growth rates. This is often overlooked. Occasionally the argument is heard that, before the introduction of the Five-Year Plans in the USSR in October, 1928, no country had experienced such rapid rates of growth. Rapid growth, it is explained, became a common phenomenon only after the

Soviet experience, not before it. This, however, is an overstatement. The Soviet experience and their loud trumpeting of it has made the world more growth conscious than it was before, but that does not mean that the Soviet Union was the first state to attain such a rate of growth.

Part of the reason why there was no proper appreciation of such growth prior to 1930 was that economists at that time were not especially concerned with growth. Therefore, as both a consequence and cause, very little work had been done in devising economic measures for growth. Such concepts as GNP and National Income were esoteric abstractions that only a few scholars bothered to contemplate. Therefore, it was only in retrospect, several years later, that economists began to discover that highly respectable growth rates were not that unusual prior to World War I. Thus, in addition to the prerevolutionary Russian rate, Germany experienced an average rate of industrial growth that was estimated at 5.5 per cent between 1888 and 1896. Sweden had a rate of 12 per cent during the same period, and Japan grew at a rate of 8.5 per cent from 1907 to 1913.[1] Even the American net national product grew at 4.6 per cent between the periods 1869-1878 and 1899-1908.[2] It is incorrect, therefore, to say that what the communists wanted to do had never been done before; it had been done even though the statistical impact was not widely understood.

Rapid rates of growth were also attained after the Revolution but before the introduction of the First Five-Year Plan. From 1920 to 1927, the rate of growth reached about 5 per cent a year. But Communist officials at the time were not especially impressed by such rates. It was, they argued, easy to grow that fast because it was relatively simple to place into operation equipment that had been dismantled, destroyed, or simply neglected during the war and the civil war that followed the Revolution from 1917 to 1921. However, by 1927-1928, the process of reconstructing the damage had been completed and the Communists feared that future expansions and growth would come only at a considerably reduced rate of speed.

[1] Gerschenkron, *op. cit.*, p. 78.
[2] Abram Bergson and Simon Kuznets, eds., *Economic Trends in the Soviet Union*. Cambridge, Mass.: Harvard University Press, 1963, p. 7.

As we saw, because he feared such a retardation in the rate of growth, Stalin subsequently ordered the collectivization of all peasant farms and the complete nationalization of all private industry. As Karcz has indicated, there is good reason to question whether such a move was necessary, especially in agriculture; here it is enough to mention that millions of lives (possibly as many as 10 million) were lost in the suffering and chaos that followed on the farms.[3] A less extreme but nonetheless unsettling disruption occurred in the cities. Despite the sudden expansion of the industrial work force and capital investment, there was no corresponding increase in sustaining facilities such as housing and consumer goods.

Now what would have happened if somehow this disruption had been avoided? Since we are speculating, let us carry our assumptions even further than this. What would have happened if the Bolsheviks had not come to power in November, 1917? In other words, let us assume that the revolutionary movement in Russia had ceased with the February Revolution of 1917. The extremists would not have taken control. Presumably this would have eliminated the civil war, collectivization, and massive nationalization, all of which were followed by waste and retardation. To some extent, the Russians have even today not fully recovered from the disruption that took place in agriculture. Without the need to backtrack and recover, perhaps a more moderate government would have done just as well. Since there would be no need to make up for lost ground, a less intensive rate of growth might have carried the economy just as far. In other words, could the USSR have developed as strong an economy as it has today with a less disruptive system of economic growth?

Without the counterrevolution and collectivization, conceivably the Russians would have had at least ten more years for growth. If so, there would have been less need for intensive growth in the years that followed. Therefore the Russians might have been able to attain the same level of economic development without so much pressure and anguish. To be fair, it must also be acknowledged that some of this extra growth might have been offset by the effects of the depression, which affected much of the rest of the world. But even then, if they

[3] Winston S. Churchill, *The Hinges of Fate,* Boston, Mass.: Houghton-Mifflin, 1950, pp. 498-499.

33

had continued their prerevolutionary expansion, the Russians might have been able to grow just as fast under an alternative economic system.

Oddly enough, although it might seem that the only question is whether or not there had to be collectivization or nationalization, it is almost equally hard to determine what the rate of economic growth actually was. Measurement of economic growth is very much influenced by the type of index weights that are used and the period of time covered. Most competent scholars, including some in the Soviet Union, agree that Soviet estimates of the growth of their GNP were highly exaggerated. If official indices were linked together, Soviet data would show that its national income has grown from 30 to 40 times since 1913. Apparently this is even too much for most Russians; so the calculation is usually broken down into two periods, 1913 to 1940 and 1940 to 1967, and figures are shown only for the more recent period of 1940 to 1967.[4] In contrast, one of the best Western estimates of Soviet economic growth by Abram Bergson of Harvard University found that the GNP of the Soviet Union grew by about 400 per cent from 1928 to 1958, or about 7 per cent per year. Subsequent estimates by Stanley Cohn show the rate of growth fell to about 5.3 per cent from 1959 to 1964.[5] There have been no Western estimates published since that time, but the average probably increased in 1965-1967 to about 6 per cent. This would make a total growth of about 650 per cent from 1928, which in turn was the year in which production reached the prewar level of 1913. This is the figure we shall use.

If we can assume that, without the counterrevolution and collectivization, the Russians would have had ten more years in which to grow, what rates of economic growth would have been necessary for the Russians to have done as well as the Soviets actually did? Let us first assume that the whole period of the 1920s and 1930s was a time of growth. Call this case *A*. There was no growth from 1940 to 1950 because of World War II and its aftermath; therefore, it does not affect our calculations. In case *B*, a stronger assumption is made that, like the United States, the USSR had no economic growth during the

[4] *Ekonomicheskaia Gazeta*, **27**, July, 1967, p. 7.
[5] "Soviet Growth Retardation: Trends in Resource Availability and Efficiency," *New Directions in the Soviet Economy*, prepared for the Joint Economic Committee, 89th Congress, 2nd session, p. 105.

first seven years of the 1930s because of the depression.[6] Actually, some countries such as Japan apparently did not suffer a fall in GNP, only a fall in the rate at which it grew. Nonetheless we shall assume in case *B* that the Russians would have lagged in the same way as the United States did.

In both case *A* and *B* we have to determine what the minimum rate of growth would have had to be in order to carry the USSR to 650 per cent of its 1913 GNP, the economic level it eventually attained in the years 1966-1967. As shown in Table 3, the Soviet Union would

TABLE 3 MULTIPLES OF GROSS NATIONAL PRODUCT POSSIBLE
WITH VARIOUS RATES OF ANNUAL GROWTH

	4%	*5%*	*5.2%*	*6%*	*6.4%*	*6.5%*
Case *A*: 1920-1940 1950-1967	4.26806	6.08136	6.52499	8.63603	9.92746	10.2785
Case *B*: 1920-1930 1937-1940 1950-1967	3.24337	4.32191	4.70813	5.74345	6.43053	6.61433

only have had to grow at a rate of 5.2 per cent since 1920 if we assume no stagnation during the depression. In case *B*, i.e., if we assume a pause for the depression, a rate just over 6.4 per cent would have been required to carry the USSR to its 1967 level.

Could the Russians have attained an average rate of growth of either 5.2 or 6.4 per cent over a 30- or 37-year period of time with a different economic system? That is the big question. In fairness, it is necessary to repeat that such sustained high growth rates prior to 1920 were not too common. Nonetheless, as we have just seen, Russia itself exceeded both rates during the decade of the 1890s and maintained about a 6 per cent rate in the ten-year period before 1914. Moreover, in the years after World War II, such high rates became much more common, and countries like Japan, West Germany, and Italy have averaged at least 5.6 per cent for about 15 years. During

[6] *The Economic Report of the President,* Washington: U.S. Government Printing Office, Jan., 1967, p. 214.

the period of 1958 to 1964, Japan reached a rate of 12 per cent.[7] Almost as impressive rates were made by such countries as Yugoslavia, Mexico, Israel, and Taiwan. Even the United States exceeded a rate of 4 per cent in the decade prior to 1967. Thus there is at least a possibility that the Russians could have achieved equally impressive rates with an alternative system.

As we have indicated, showing that something can be done is not the same as proving it would have been done. Moreover, it is also necessary to show that such rates can be sustained for a period as long as 30, not to mention 37, years. Our evidence on this is inconclusive. Yet it is interesting to compare the relative growth of a country like Japan over the same period of time. Precise statistical data is difficult to find. But some very rough calculations indicate that the growth of *per capita GNP* from 1913 to 1964 was practically the same in Japan and the USSR.[8] The implication is that Japan through two wars and a depression has grown at least as fast as the USSR.

The purpose here is not as extreme as the above paragraph suggests. It is not necessary to show that a particular country has grown five-tenths of a per cent faster than another. Instead, it is enough to suggest that the Soviet experience, although an impressive one, is not really that unique. Indeed, another approach to economic development may have been even more productive. Certainly it might have been less destructive.

REALITY: *High rates of economic growth have been attained by many countries, and by some over a prolonged period of time. Soviet economic growth over the last fifty years has been impressive, but there is good reason to believe that an alternative approach might have brought about a comparable result.*

[7] Stanley Cohn, p. 105.

[8] Per capita income increased by slightly more than 3.5 times in both Japan and the USSR. Data for Japan is taken from the following sources: for the years 1913 to 1930 from Simon Kuznets, *Economic Growth: Brazil, India, Japan,* Durham, N.C.: Duke University Press, 1955, p. 169; the years 1930 to 1958 from Hitotsubashi Daigaku Keizaikenkyusho, ed., *Kaisetsu Nihon Keizai Tokei.* Tokyo: Iwanami Shoten, 1961. (I am indebted to Yashusi Toda for drawing this source to my attention.) The years 1959 to 1964 from Stanley Cohn, p. 105. Data for the Soviet Union: for the years 1913 to 1928 from Abram Bergson and Simon Kuznets, eds., *Economic Trends in the Soviet Union,* Cambridge, Mass.: Harvard University Press, 1963, p. 337; the years 1958 to 1964 from Stanley Cohn, p. 105.

PART II

Economic
Freedom
and Totalitarianism
in the Soviet Union

CHAPTER 5

MYTH: *The Soviet economic system is totalitarian and by nature it is a slave state.*

Because so much of what we read and hear about the USSR has come to us through the framework of the cold war, some of us have developed enormous misconceptions. But to be fair, to some extent our lack of knowledge is a reflection of our general ignorance of foreign lands and customs. As opposed to most European citizens who are surrounded by several countries all with different languages, we are surrounded by two oceans, two countries and one different language. Because of our protected geographical situation, we feel less need to concern ourselves with other countries.[1] But, when thinking about the USSR, it is not just that we are generally unaware of foreign customs. There is also the fact that the USSR has been considered our prime antagonist for the last twenty years. Since it usually is bad form to think too well of your enemy and because there is much that deserves criticism, unpleasant aspects of Soviet life tend to be exaggerated and sometimes publicized even when corrective reforms may have been introduced.

Before considering areas where freedoms have indeed been limited in the Soviet Union, we shall first examine conditions which are not as bad as is sometimes charged.

[1] Because of similar isolation, the Russians, like the Americans, also tend to be more self-centered.

39

One of the most extreme indictments of the present Soviet system is that it is a totalitarian slave state. What exactly is meant by this charge is not always made clear. In fact, the tendency to generalize without being specific is a common shortcoming of those who feel most strongly about the Soviet Union. What is the basis for such a claim?

The charge of totalitarian slavery usually derives from two sources: (1) the political conditions that prevail whenever one party exercises monopoly control and (2) the traumatic terror which existed under Stalin. The political conditions that develop when one party forbids the existence of other parties usually turn out to be deplorable. No matter what the rationalization is for one party or how much truth there may be to the argument that the two-party system does not offer any real choice, a one-party system eliminates any prospect of dissent. It is hard if not impossible to find a political system with one party where disagreement or criticism is tolerated, much less encouraged. Despite the best of initial intentions, the ruling authorities come to feel that criticism only rocks the boat and makes political and economic navigation all the more difficult. Regardless of the fact that the waves may be generated by faulty steering, most captains tend to blame someone else other than themselves for their problems. Moreover, they fear that criticism of their work may detract from its eventual success. Ultimately criticism of the means and sometimes of the ends is discouraged and often prohibited. Gradually not only is control exercised through the political party, but the press, radio, and television. It is even difficult, if not impossible, to acquire a private mimeograph, not to mention a Xerox machine.

The existence of such controls is usually recognized and acknowledged by perceptive and candid Russians and East Europeans. Occasionally they express their feelings in anecdotal forms. Thus, when an American tried to prove his freedom by boasting that he could picket and shout in front of the White House that Lyndon Johnson was a political misfit and that the American democratic system should be overthrown, his Russian host wryly boasted that he could do the same thing in the Soviet Union. Any time he wanted to, he replied, he too could go to the Kremlin and picket and shout that President Johnson was a political misfit and that the American democratic system should be overthrown!

Sensitive Russians also resent their inability to travel abroad freely.

Passports for overseas travel are issued only after a thorough security check. And even then private travel, especially to countries outside of Eastern Europe, is unusual because the Russian ruble is not legally convertible and few, if any, Russians are provided with foreign exchange to spend abroad. But, while it may be hard to obtain a passport for foreign travel, every Soviet citizen must carry an Internal Passport. He must be in possession of this passport at all times. When he leaves town for any protracted period of time, he usually must notify the police in his hometown as well as in the community which he is visiting.

The police themselves have been the target of bitter criticism. While fear of the secret police continues today, the worst excesses occurred under Stalin. The midnight knocks on the door, periodic purges, and overflowing concentration camps were a part of the daily routine. For most Russians today, the 30-year period from the mid-1920s until the mid-1950s seems like a long nightmare that could never happen again. Still, there were those who, in 1920, said the excesses of the Czar would never recur again either.

Job Freedom

Most of the above criticisms, while serious enough, primarily affect the political sphere. Whatever the aftereffects of the Stalinist period and the continuing intimidation within the present political system, conditions in the political sphere have markedly improved. But the political shortcomings notwithstanding, the charge that the Soviet Union is a slave state usually refers to economic circumstances. In its extreme form, the slave state condition was used to describe the fact that a portion of Soviet productive work was performed by concentration camp inmates. Under Stalin this charge did have considerable truth to it. Since the mid-1950s, however, most of these camps have been emptied. In any event, there are few political prisoners left in the camps that remain, whereas, under Stalin, political prisoners often constituted the bulk of the inmates.[2]

[2] For a depressingly vivid description of life in such a camp, see Alexander Solzhenitsyn, *A Day in the Life of Ivan Denisovich.* New York: Frederick A. Praeger, Inc., 1963.

The slave state charge also stemmed from the Soviet practice of determining job assignments. This practice began in the 1930s when collective farms were ordered to supply quotas of laborers for work in urban factories. After the start of World War II, Stalin ordered additional regulations for labor. Labor Reserve Schools were established for young people who were then drafted into various trades. Moreover, orders were issued in 1940 that no one could leave his job without permission. This was to prevent desertion and chaos during the expected war. But it also had the effect of enserfing the worker. Even though enforcement of these laws was reduced gradually after the war, these "emergency measures" were not officially abolished until April 25, 1956, three years after Stalin's death.[3]

Other measures were decreed to regulate the Soviet worker, but the effect was not as sweeping. Because of the shortage of labor and the problems that the predominantly rural population had in adjusting to an industrial way of life, labor turnover was very high. To limit this labor flow, the government issued compulsory Labor Books in 1938. Although there was considerable disregard for the law, officially each worker was supposed to hand over his Labor Book to his employer. The worker would then be unable to take a new job until he had given his employer a month's notice. When the Labor Book had been properly certified by his old employer, the worker could then move to his next job. A persistent labor shortage forced most plant managers to overlook minor irregularities when their need for more employees was great enough. Soviet workers still have Labor Books today, but now they need give only two weeks' notice. Although Labor Books do constitute a restriction on the worker, it is an exaggeration to describe this as a form of slave labor.

In addition to the existence of the Labor Book, the only other interference with job choice that was not eliminated in 1956 is the practice of work placement after graduation from a technical school. In exchange for a tuition-free college or technical-school education, each Soviet student agrees to accept a job assignment in his field for three years. This practice dates from the late 1920s. In many ways, it resembles the commitment of those who accept appointment at the

[3] Emily Clark Brown, *Soviet Trade Unions and Labor Relations.* Cambridge, Mass.: Harvard University Press, 1966, p. 16.

42

various military academies in the United States. Each cadet promises that, in exchange for an expense-paid education, he will accept government duty for a specified period of time. Just as in the United States, Soviet students can obtain a release from their obligation, but again it hardly seems appropriate to consider such service as slavery. Thus the Soviet worker today has virtually complete freedom of job choice with only minimal restrictions.

Another indication of the improvement in the working conditions of the Soviet laborer that has occurred in the last few years is the introduction of the shorter work week. Until 1966, most Soviet employees worked six days a week. This was made up of five seven-hour days and one six-hour day for a total of 41 hours. The effect, however, was to make Sunday the only free day. In April, 1966, Kosygin announced the adoption of a five-day week. Each worker must still work 41 hours, but he now has two complete days free for himself, which creates a significant increase in leisure time.

Education

Having just mentioned tuition-free education, it seems appropriate here to say something more about education in the Soviet Union.[4] School attendance is compulsory through the eighth grade. By 1970, this will be extended to include the tenth grade. All education is tuition-free. Moreover, most undergraduate students receive a small stipend from the state. Normally it is not enough to live well, but this is a remarkable innovation. Of course, just because study in the university and technical institutes is free does not mean that everyone who wants to is able to enroll. As in most other West European countries, there is a serious space shortage in Russian educational institutions. Only in the United States is there the feeling that anyone who wants to go to college should be provided with a space and often financial support. There simply are not enough universities in the USSR and elsewhere to satisfy the need of those who would like to

[4] For a detailed study, see Nicholas DeWitt, *Education and Professional Employment in the USSR*. Washington, D.C.: U.S. Government Printing Office, 1961.

43

go. Consequently, application requirements in the USSR are very rigorous, and many students are not able to attend any institution of higher learning or they are diverted to technical institutes, which still may be very good. In fact, in contrast to American practice, the Russians tend to give preference to technical training. Thus, even though there are about 1.5 million more students in American institutions of advanced learning than there are in the Soviet Union, Soviet schools graduate more engineers each year than do American schools.

The school curriculum in the Soviet Union includes a good deal of political propaganda which every student must take. From primary school through college the student is confronted with a constant diet of Marx and Lenin. As with any dish which is served day after day, the student inevitably acquires a distinct distaste for it. In other courses as well, there is often a persistent ideological tone to the material that is presented. Just as it is ill-advised to stand in front of the Kremlin and criticize without restraint, so it would be unwise in the university. Yet there is criticism in academic circles, and this is a sign of progress. The day of the "teach in," the "sit in," not to mention "course evaluations" will be a long time in coming to the Soviet university. But their absence and the presence of Marxist requirements hardly warrants the label "slave state in education."

Academic freedom, it is not, but there does seem to be a remarkable emphasis on education. Any society that can wipe out illiteracy, provide compulsory education at the primary-school level, and arrange free, though limited, education at the advanced level deserves praise regardless of the shortcomings.

Medical Care

Similarly, Soviet medical care is imperfect but nonetheless a major improvement over prerevolutionary conditions. Now that private insurance programs like Blue Cross provide financial protection for a large number of American families, Medicare underwrites the usually extensive needs of the elderly, and Medicaid finances the needs of the indigent, the problems of financing medical care in this country do not seem as pressing as they once were. But until the 1960s medical costs were a major uncertainty which faced almost every American family. Many were the families who found their entire life savings exhausted in the care of some member of the family. Now that the likelihood of such an occurrence has been lessened by both private and public medical plans, we no longer worry so much about medical emergencies. Therefore now it is a little hard to appreciate just how significant it was for the Russians to announce shortly after the revolution that henceforth qualified medical care was to be free.[5]

Anyone who has ever had even an introductory course in economics knows that a sudden decree that complete medical care will be free to all citizens next January 4 cannot be immediately or effectively implemented especially in a poor country. At any one time, there are only so many medical facilities and personnel available, and they can be spread out only so far. Even a little stretching runs the risk that the quality of care will suffer in the process. Inevitably, this is what happened in the Soviet Union. Even 50 years after the revolution they have not completely recovered. However, there is a trade-off between the knowledge that everyone can have a minimal amount of care and the realization that some may not be able to afford any care at all.

The beginning student of economics also knows that even bad medical care costs something. No matter how nice the sentiment, nobody gets anything for nothing. Even if the Soviet citizen pays nothing directly for his care, he, like the American on Medicare, must ultimately pay for what care he or his neighbor receives by means of a tax. Many people resent having the government make decisions of this sort for them. There is also resentment over the fact that those with personal and political connections usually are able to obtain better service and care for themselves from better doctors. For example, those in the Kremlin have their own special medical facilities and staff. But whatever the intrusion of the government into this additional realm of activity, there is still something heartless about restricting medical care only to those who can afford it as is sometimes the case in some other countries.

Universal medical care in the Soviet Union therefore was a progressive step. Undoubtedly it had an effect on the other countries of

[5] Mark G. Field, *Soviet Socialized Medicine.* New York: The Free Press, 1967, p. 60.

the world and stimulated similar movements elsewhere. At the same time there seems little question that the quality of Soviet care often leaves much to be desired. Fortunately those who demand better care in the Soviet Union and can pay for it can have their own private physicians. With such a combination of medical care for all and maximum care for those who can afford it, the Russians deserve more praise than criticism for their medical system.

Social Security

In addition to medical care, the Russians provide other forms of social security. The Russians have been extremely proud of their program for retirement income and expense-free vacations. Of course, since the average *monthly* wage was only $110 in 1966, average pensions, which are only a portion of the original wage, were considerably smaller. Consequently, retirement does not bring a flood of wealth. Moreover, since there are only so many resort areas and only so many hotel rooms in these areas, there is simply not enough room to provide a place in a vacation resort for every Soviet worker even during the off season. Consequently, the tendency is to send those workers with seniority or the proper connections to the better resorts at the right time of year. Nonetheless, the Russians are proud of their system because it does provide them with a minimum level of financial protection and hope of receiving some sort of vacation even if not the best. Given free medical care and a basic, if not adequate, pension plan, most Russians find themselves relieved of the uncertainties of old age that, until a few years ago, plagued older citizens in the United States.

As part of their social benefit scheme, the Russians have also developed an elaborate and extensive system of children's camps. Such camps are located throughout the country and are often sponsored by the local trade unions. They are well run and intelligently administered. Compared with the adult camps, there is a larger number of children's camps and therefore more children can be accommodated.

Although the social benefit picture is an appealing one, as always there are shortcomings that the casual observer might miss. For example, until 1965, such benefits in the USSR were only made available to urban residents. In effect, this excluded the inhabitants of the collective farms who constitute more than 25 per cent of the population. Only if their own collective farm had its own plan would they have any protection. Since the peasantry generally has not been favored as much as the urban population, there were very few collective farms that had such programs. Moreover, since the collective farmers tend to have lower incomes than urban residents (in 1965 the average wage per collective farmer was less than 50 per cent of that of the average urban resident),[6] peasants are the ones who have the greatest need for such a program. The misery and despair facing the average peasant, both retired and active, is dramatically illustrated in the recent Soviet novel *A Day in the New Life* by Fydor Abramov in which the peasants on pension almost starve for lack of help and young peasants refuse work because of the low pay. Recognizing the inequity of such situations, the Soviet government finally decided that a pension program should also be made available for the peasants. Of course its provisions are less favorable than those for urban workers, but at least a major inequity has been corrected.

Interestingly enough, one important form of social benefit is entirely absent in the Soviet program. There is no provision for unemployment compensation. Replying to the shocked response of Western observers about this omission, most Russians proudly declare that there is no unemployment compensation in the USSR because there is no unemployment! Like almost everything else in the USSR, this is part myth and part reality. Unquestionably there is a serious labor shortage in the Soviet Union. For decades now, there has been a very marked shortage of manpower in both skilled and unskilled job classifications. True enough, many of these vacancies have been in less desirable areas such as the Far North of the USSR or in Siberia. But the fact remains that anyone who wants a job should have been able to find a position somewhere even if it is not exactly in the applicant's specialty. Thus the overwhelming majority of Russians have never known what it is like to be unemployed or worry about having a job a year from now. This in itself may provide more important psychological security than all of the other social benefits combined. It is hard to

[6] Soviet News, May 23, 1967, pp. 98-99.

describe the fears and feelings of inadequacy that plague a person looking for a job. Whether it is due to a person's incompetence or to some factor outside the control of the individual, there is little in the world that is as humiliating or depressing.

But the situation in the USSR is not as idyllic as the preceding paragraph would indicate, either from the personal or nation's point of view. First of all, there is frictional unemployment just as there must be in any industrialized state. Under the best of circumstances, there are seasonal variations in production as well as technological changes. For example, canning plants all over the world are busy during the harvest season and idle the rest of the year, just as swimsuit manufacturers have production schedules that are considerably different from those of snowshoe producers. Similarly factories making piano-roll players have to adjust to changed demand conditions just as a factory making pocket watches. In the same way a grocery store may suddenly find all its customers have moved when the apartments surrounding it are demolished for some new industrial project. Of necessity such adjustments require the cessation of productive activity. This in turn involves the firing or at best the temporary displacement of at least a portion of the work force.

In addition to structural changes in the productive life of an enterprise, there are also personal and even political conflicts that arise from time to time. Although the worker is supposed to be protected from the personal whims of his foreman, there are occasions when the worker is fired and finds it impossible to appeal the decision. The same situation sometimes arises because of political or religious antagonisms. I have personally met a Soviet citizen who was fired from her job for such reasons and was unable to find alternative employment for a year and a half. Of course, she could always have taken a job as a scrubwoman or skilled engineer, but she was a schoolteacher and wanted something in her general field of training. In other words, her problem was almost like that of an unemployed person anyplace else in the world. If anything her problem was somewhat more acute because, as she explained, there was no unemployment compensation available to tide her over until she could find a new job. Similarly this is the dilemma of anyone in the Soviet system who finds himself unemployed despite the state regulations which proclaim that it cannot happen. Implicit in all of this is the knowledge that someone who has indulged in serious political indiscretions may find himself unable to obtain work. Clearly this can be as disquieting for the individual as being unemployed. The Russian novelist, Alexander Solzhenitsyn, apparently found himself in exactly such a situation during the summer of 1967 when he was unable to publish his work.[7]

For the most part, however, very few Russians find themselves with a problem like Solzhenitsyn's or that of my schoolteacher friend. The average Russian, as is true of most people of the world, tends to lead a straight and narrow life. Therefore, as indicated earlier, he is spared the consequences or the fear of unemployment.

Oddly enough, however, some Soviet economists are coming to recognize that virtually full employment may not be all to the good. Because of the fuss that is made about the absence of unemployment, many Soviet managers are reluctant to fire inefficient employees. Similarly, productive innovations are sometimes frustrated because of the realization that employees will be displaced in the process. Some factories find they bear responsibility for the well-being of their employees and must find them alternative positions before they can be dropped from the payroll. As a result, many managers decide it is cheaper to keep such people on the staff than devote time and effort to running their own employment office. Such practices also give rise to an attitude that labor need not be especially productive. Soviet managers have accustomed themselves to seeing all kinds of auxiliary personnel around such as floor *dezhurnia* (receptionists) and other superfluous drones. Consequently, many managers fail to realize how much lower production costs would be if such people were removed. Of course, if such a concept became widely accepted, it might give rise to overt unemployment. As it is now, unlike Poland and Yugoslavia where the unemployment problem is in the open for all to see, most of the problem is hidden in the Soviet Union through the expedient of disguised unemployment.

Of course, the cost of sustaining such nonproductive workers may still be less than the costs of operating a program of unemployment compensation. However, there are some Russian economists who have made just such a calculation and have apparently concluded

[7] *New York Times,* June 5, 1967, p. 1.

exactly the opposite. They argue that the cost of unemployment compensation would be more than offset by efficiencies that could then be made in industrial productivity. With a minimum of doubletalk, economists like Manevich, Iagodkin, and Maslova have pointed to the growing surplus of workers due to such factors as automation and the postwar baby boom.[8] To solve such problems and to make it easy for factory managers who want to reduce the size of their staffs, Manevich suggests that the state set up a system of unemployment compensation supplemented by a state-run employment agency. This would pay for itself by making it possible to reduce the costs of production.

The calls for action have obviously had some impact. In the hope that managers will turn loose some of their drones and other unproductive employees, the first step toward the formation of labor exchanges was made in 1967. State Committees on the Use of Labor Resources were established for the purpose of providing better mobility of labor and of paving the path for automation.[9] At the same time, several factory managers have decided to proceed with the task of trimming their work forces regardless of the lack of unemployment compensation. As part of the new economic reforms, which will be considered in more detail in Chapter 9, enterprise managers are trying to reduce their costs in the hope that they and the remaining employees would then be eligible for higher bonuses.[10] This has won the applause of the Soviet government, but it has been embarrassing from an ideological point of view.

Standard of Living

Precise statements about the comparative standard of living in different countries must be regarded with considerable caution. There is no acceptable way to allow for the fact that the well-equipped Russian home has a samovar which would be completely out of place in the up-to-date American home. Similarly, the methodical statisti-

[8] *Voprosy Ekonomiki*, June, 1965, pp. 27, 31.
[9] *Pravda*, Feb. 18, 1967, p. 4; *Trud*, May 6, 1967, p. 2.
[10] *Planovoe Khoziastvo*, Apr., 1967, p. 8.

cian would be shocked to discover that, even though only one or two Russian homes have pop-up toasters, this is not necessarily a sign of a lower standard of living. The better explanation is that the average Russian has no use for a toaster because toasters are meant primarily for people who eat uniformly sliced white bread. The Russians, however, prefer dark bread, and, like most Europeans, they buy their bread unsliced by the loaf.[11] The point is, of course, that cultural tastes are difficult if not impossible to incorporate in any such study. Therefore, the presence or absence of a particular item does not necessarily imply a lower standard of living.

Yet, as difficult as it is to obtain precise or even imprecise comparisons, the Russian standard of living has risen significantly since 1954. Clearly, the average Russian is not wallowing in a condition of poverty, as some critics in this country charge. It is true that, in 1952, the real wage income of the urban consumer was still below that of 1928, the year of collectivization, and that the peasant was in considerably poorer condition.[12] It is also true that the standard of living of the rural population did not reach precollectivization levels until several years after Stalin's death. Nonetheless, improvements have been constant since then. A rough indication of the progress that has been made is that the average wage of the Soviet industrial worker has risen from about $80 a month in 1955 to about $110 a month by 1966. This is a little over 2.5 per cent a year. Kosygin has promised that, by 1970, the average wage will rise to $126 a month, an increase of almost 4 per cent a year. The minimum wage was increased from $50 to $66 a month as of January, 1968. In any case, we shall see that, once the consumer is able to move above the level at which his daily needs are provided for, the increase in living conditions improves at a multiple rate. Living conditions in the Soviet Union are still considerably below those in the United States (in a week the average American factory worker earns almost as much as the average Russian factory worker earns in a month), but they are

[11] That the Russians do not always appreciate the subtleties involved is indicated in a Russian attempt to illustrate a toaster for the Soviet consumer in one of their magazines. The toaster is jammed with two roughly cut slices of dark bread. *Novye Tovary,* Nov., 1959, p. 29.

[12] Janet Chapman, *Real Wages in Soviet Russia Since 1928.* Cambridge, Mass.: Harvard University Press, 1963, p. 166.

not too far from those of some of the poorer West European countries.

The ideal in the United States still seems to be a home in the suburbs, but, for the average Russian, it is to have his private apartment with private bath and kitchen. Because Stalin permitted few of the country's resources to be directed toward housing construction, this ideal has been beyond the reach of most Russian citizens. The vast majority of Moscovites, for example, have had to share apartments. Until recently, this meant that each family was assigned its own room with two or three others in the same apartment suite. In other words, all families shared the kitchen and toilet. Naturally, this was an extremely unpleasant situation and precluded virtually all privacy. This was to some extent conscious state policy, but it was very unpopular. Recognizing the unpleasantness of the housing situation, Khrushchev and his successors embarked on a vast housing program that saw the construction of as many as 2,711,000 apartments in 1959.[13] As part of the general slowdown in economic growth mentioned earlier in Chapter 4, apartment construction fell off in subsequent years. In 1964, the Russians were able to complete only 2,184,000 apartments, still an impressive number but over 500,000 fewer than in 1959. Fortunately construction increased again in 1965 and 1966, but the Russians were still far below their peak of 1959.

The rapid expansion in apartment construction has gone a long way in providing more room and privacy. This has meant immense improvement in the daily lives of millions of people. However, again there is more to the situation than immediately meets the eye. Construction standards in the Soviet Union are very poor by Western norms. New buildings often look old after no more than a year. The finishing is bad and the workmanship is generally shoddy. (We shall have more to say about this in Chapter 9 on reform.) Like tree specialists, Russian specialists can often tell the age of Soviet-built buildings by counting the different shades of brick on the exterior surface of a building. After the spring thaw each year, the poor cement cracks on many buildings and the bricks fall down. Each year, a slightly different shade of brick replacement seems to be used. Thus,

[13] *Narodnoe Khoziaistvo SSSR v 1965 Godu.* Tsentral'noe Statisticheskoe Upravlenie, Moscow, Gosstatizdat, 1966, p. 611. (Hereafter referred to as *Nar. Khoz.* and the appropriate year.)

like the number of rings in a tree stump, the different shades of brick indicate how old the building is. Many Soviet buildings have a wire fence extending out above the first floor as a safety precaution to protect passing pedestrians.

Part of the speedup in construction (until 1956 only 1,548,000 apartments were being built a year, which was a million less than were constructed in the 1959 peak) was made possible by the use of prefabricated production techniques. Huge trucks and cranes would assemble apartment units on location. In some experiments, an entire apartment unit would be prepared in advance and lifted intact onto its assigned place. This apparently proved to be less efficient than working with smaller prepacked sections. Moreover, the poorer Soviet construction procedures meant that all the parts did not fit together properly, which made for more circulation than was intended. Although the construction of more than 2 million apartments a year is not to be minimized by snide comments about construction standards which in any case have improved in recent years, important differences do exist between what is expected by the Soviet apartment dwellers and their American counterparts. For example, there were only two Soviet bathtubs manufactured for every three Soviet apartments constructed in 1965. This is a considerable improvement over 1960 when the rate was about 1 to 4. At that time only 46.2 per cent of all the apartments in Moscow itself had baths or showers.[14] The figure for the rest of the country was accordingly much lower.

With more space available and with higher incomes, the Russians have finally been able to afford and store consumer appliances. More important, the Soviet government has made rapid strides in providing an increased number of appliances in the retail stores to satisfy the pent-up demand. The production of appliances such as refrigerators, washing machines, and television sets has grown at a phenomenal pace, as Table 4 shows. The extreme case is the production of refrigerators which doubled in the two-year period from 1964 to 1966. Nevertheless the demand for refrigerators and washing machines and, to a lesser extent, television sets and vacuum cleaners is still unsatisfied. According to a market survey of the Soviet government in late 1965, the demand for refrigerators was 10 times the supply and the

[14] *Nar. Khoz., 1965,* pp. 221, 611; V. G. Kriazhev, *Vnerabochee Vremia i Spera Obsluzhivaniia.* Moscow, Ekonomika, 1966, p. 73.

TABLE 4 PRODUCTION OF MAJOR APPLIANCES IN THE USSR AND
THE UNITED STATES
in millions

	Soviet Production						United States Production
	1958	1960	1962	1964	1966	Plan 1970	1966
Automobiles	0.122	0.139	0.166	0.185	0.230	0.7-0.8	9.0
Bicycles	3.7	2.8	3.1	3.6	4.0		
Radios and phono-graphs	3.9	4.2	4.3	4.8	5.8	7.5-8.0	19.0
Refrigerators	0.4	0.5	0.8	1.1	2.2	5.4-5.6	6.0 (including 1.1 freezers)
Sewing machines	2.7	3.1	3.3	1.6	1.0		
Television sets	1.0	1.7	2.2	2.9	4.4	7.5-7.7	12.3 (including 5.1 in color)
Cameras	1.5	1.8	1.3	1.2	1.4		
Vacuum cleaners	0.2	0.5	0.6	0.8	0.9		5.5
Washing machines	0.5	0.9	1.8	2.9	3.9		4.5
Watches	24.8	26.0	26.1	28.7	32.4		

Sources: 1958-1964, *Nar. Khoz.*, *1965*, Moscow, 1966. *Nar. Khoz.*, *1963*.
1966, *Ekonomicheskaia Gazeta*, **5**, Feb., 1967, p. 3.
1970, *Ekonomicheskaia Gazeta*, **15**, Apr., 1966, p. 12.
1966 (United States), *Electrical Merchandising Week*, Jan., 1967, pp. 19-25. U.S. Bureau of the Census, *Statistical Abstract of the United States: 1966*, 87th ed., 1966, p. 339.

demand for washing machines was double the supply.[15] Consequently, 78 per cent of the people who went shopping for a refrigerator walked out of the store empty-handed because there were no refrigerators available for sale. Similarly unsatisfied washing-machine shoppers made no purchase approximately 60 per cent of the time because there were no washing machines in stock.

[15] *Sovetskaia Torgovlia,* Apr., 1967, p. 19.

Those who were lucky enough to find and buy the appliance they were seeking discovered, of course, that the quality of the appliance generally left much to be desired. The continuing rapid growth in production has nonetheless made it possible for the Russians to produce almost as many washing machines per year as we do. Conceivably, they may soon outproduce us in the manufacture of refrigerators and some other appliances. It must be emphasized, however, that a Soviet washer is normally not semiautomatic, whereas about 85 per cent of the washers produced in the United States are. Nonetheless, the purchase of a washer or other appliance where there was none before is a major improvement. Many Soviet families have heretofore been living on a loaf-to-loaf basis; the bulk of their purchases have been for the purpose of sustaining life. Until the late 1950s there was little income left over for consumer goods of a more durable nature. Then the Soviet consumer's income increased so that he was able to spend money on products that generated enjoyment long after the initial purchase. Unlike a loaf of bread, a Soviet refrigerator provides consumptive pleasure for more than a few days. Thus, an index of consumption which measures only current sales understates the enormous improvement that is taking place in the daily life of the Soviet consumer.[16]

Although the improvement in Soviet living conditions has been impressive and although production levels of various appliances may soon parallel or even exceed American output, this in itself does not mean that the Russians are now as well off as the Americans. Just as the purchase of an appliance today means that the use of it will continue for several years in the future, so the purchase of an appliance several years ago means that enjoyment of it is probably continuing today. Even if Americans buy fewer appliances in any one year, the more important question is how many do they have on hand from past years. In other words, what is the size of the stock of a country's appliances that is providing a continuing source of enjoyment? Except for new types of appliances like dishwashers and air conditioners (which are for all intents and purposes just being dis-

[16] In a sense, every time an appliance is sold, the national income of a country is increased for several years in the future, whereas the sale of a loaf of bread increases the national income only in the year it is sold. Yet the impact of the appliance is counted once, the same as the loaf of bread.

covered in the USSR), production in the United States of appliances like refrigerators, washing machines, and vacuum cleaners is not now experiencing the astronomical growth that has occurred recently in the Soviet Union. However, American factories have produced these appliances in large quantities for a long time. Consequently, even if no discount is made for the poorer quality and poorer service of the

TABLE 5   CONSUMER DURABLES IN THE USSR AND THE UNITED STATES

	Soviet Union				United States
	Percentage of Russian Families with Appliance			Stock of Appliance, 1965,	Homes with Appliance, 1966,
	1951 (1)	1965 (2)	1970 Plan (3)	millions (4)	millions (5)
Automobiles		1		1.5	46. (Total stock, 75)
Bicycles	5	54	60	38.	
Camera equipment	4	22	25	13.-15.	
Radios and phonographs	6	61	72	42.	58.6
Refrigerators		11	35	7.5	58.6 (including 15.5 freezers)
Sewing machines	14	52	56	33.-36.	
Television sets		26	56	18.	57.6 (including 8.8 in color)
Vacuum cleaners				5.	
Washing machines		21	50	14.	51.9

Sources: (1) Sovetskaia Torgovlia, June, 1967, p. 5.
       (2) Sovetskaia Torgovlia, June, 1967, p. 5.
       (3) Sovetskaia Torgovlia, June, 1967, p. 5.
       (4) Sovetskaia Torgovlia, June, 1966, p. 19. (70 million families x (2)) Nar. Khoz., 1965, p. 20.
       (5) Electrical Merchandising Week, Jan., 1967, pp. 19-25. U.S. Bureau of the Census, Statistical Abstract of the United States: 1966, 87th ed., 1966, p. 339.

Soviet goods, the number of American households with such appliances at the present time is considerably higher than it is for the 70 million families in the USSR. See Table 5. It will, moreover, remain that way even after the conclusion of the Five-Year Plan in December, 1970. By this standard, the Russians have a long way to go before they can enjoy the pleasures presently available to the American family.

Automobiles

If the analysis is extended to include automobiles, the contrast is even sharper. In 1966, only 230,000 automobiles were produced in the Soviet Union. Furthermore, until recently production has grown at a considerably more moderate rate than that for refrigerators and washing machines. Production has seldom increased more than 15 per cent a year, and, in 1959, it grew by little more than 1 per cent. The big news, of course, is that production is to soar to four times present production levels, that is, to between 700,000 and 800,000 autos a year by 1971. To bring about such a massive increase, the Russians have contracted with Fiat of Italy to build a new plant and with Renault of France to upgrade some of the existing facilities.

Production of automobiles in the United States, by contrast, exceeded nine million in both 1965 and 1966. Those who have experienced rush hour traffic know this is not an unmixed blessing. But, whatever its shortcomings, the auto is a way of life in the United States. Over 75 million cars were registered in the United States in 1965, and figures for 1961 indicate that over 76 per cent of American families had their own car.[17] In 1967, there was approximately one car for every 3½ people. Estimates on the stock of cars in the USSR are much harder to find, but it seems doubtful that it could be more than 1.5 million. Since the majority of Russian autos are owned by the state, it is unlikely that more than 1 per cent of all Soviet families have their own car at present. Of course, as always,

[17] U.S. Bureau of the Census, *Statistical Abstract of the United States: 1966,* 87th ed., Washington, D.C., 1966, p. 339.

the prospects for the future are better, but this time there does seem to be some ground for this hope.

Although Soviet consumption levels have a long way to go before they match American levels, there is considerable evidence that the Soviet consumer is being provided a wider and wider choice of goods. This should help to expose another myth, that there is no consumer sovereignty in the Soviet Union. It is clear the consumer does not have complete control over what is made available to him since he still has to wait two years for a refrigerator or an automobile, but nonetheless the Soviet consumer has an influence. We shall see in Chapter 9 just how disruptive an influence the Soviet consumer and his changing tastes have become. Short of a major political catastrophe, it is hard to see how the Soviet government can ever return to the days of the 1930s to 1940s and early 1950s when the demands of the Soviet consumer were frequently brushed aside or ignored. Now the Soviet Union has not only committed itself to spending more than $1 billion in foreign exchange on grain when it needs it, but it also imports close to $1 billion a year in nonfood goods for the consumer. Even though the bulk of it comes from other communist countries, this is a policy that Stalin would have taken only reluctantly if at all.

Travel

Another area of liberalization, perhaps of even more long-run significance, is the increased freedom to travel. Lest this be misunderstood, only a small number of Soviet citizens a year are normally permitted to go beyond the borders of the communist bloc of countries. The majority still find it impossible to move beyond the frontier of the USSR itself. Yet each year more and more are allowed to venture outside the country. Most are sent out on some specific assignment such as business or foreign aid. Yet a select few are even permitted to explore abroad as semitourists. An overseas traveler must usually leave a form of deposit at home like a wife or child, and usually he must travel in a supervised group. Nonetheless it is becoming less and less of a surprise to find a Soviet citizen traveling abroad by himself. Usually such a person is highly trusted, but such permissiveness was unheard of a decade or so ago.

Almost of equal significance is the decision to encourage the visit of foreigners to the Soviet Union. Until 1957, it was virtually impossible for an ordinary foreigner to obtain permission to pass through the Soviet Union. Since then the tourist policy has been reversed, and now a major effort is being made to attract visitors. For the most part, foreign visitors are sought more for the foreign currency they bring with them than for their embarrassing questions. But the one cannot be separated from the other.

An especially important part of this influx has affected Soviet educational institutions. Although the foreign students are there to learn, they are also able to teach. Because they have seen the outside world and because they are brought into contact with the future educated elite of the Soviet Union, foreign students are able to convey some sense of life outside the USSR to one of the most important segments of the Soviet population. The exchange students from the United States and Western Europe have been very important in this sense.

Altogether in 1967, there were 23,500 foreign students in attendance at Soviet educational institutions. About 11,000 of these were from the developing countries, and they, too, help to bring in thoughts from the outside world.

It should be obvious that the Russians bring in students and tourists with the aim of impressing them with Soviet forms of life and institutions. Undoubtedly some leave highly taken with what they see. At the same time the exposure to foreign students and visitors seems to have had a much greater impact on the Russians. Consequently the effect of both visitors to the USSR and visitors from the USSR has been to open the vista of the average Russian to the world around him. Although this may make him more aware of the differences which exist between himself and the rest of the world and therefore frustrate him, the long-run effect is positive. The knowledge of what might be leads him to push for more of the rights and goods that heretofore have been denied him.

Another area where the Russians have made impressive progress is in their attitude toward women. Even if they were forced into it by economic necessity because of a shortage of labor, the Russians have made very intensive use of their women. Entrance into higher education and the professions is not only tolerated, it is encouraged. Women are found in the most unexpected fields, from high energy physics to geological exploration. More than half of the doctors in the USSR are women. There are very few young women whose only occupation is that of a housewife. (This is one advantage of the apartment shortage; there is less area to clean.)

But it would be wrong to exaggerate the effect of female equality. It should be kept in mind that, while all fields are open to women, relatively few women seem to be able to reach the top. Even in medicine, the chief surgeons and the most important doctors and researchers are men. Moreover, equality for women not only means privilege, it also means drudgery. Thus Russian women can be seen doing the most menial labor. I have taken pictures of Soviet women repairing railroad tracks or making heavy repairs on asphalt roads. In both instances, the driver of the truck in the first case and the driver of the steam roller in the second case were men. Women in the Soviet Union do a good portion of the unskilled work which in this country generally seems the domain of minority groups. Most Russian women must also tend an apartment and a family but without all the gadgets that save so much time in the West. But despite the unpleasant side, the women in Russia do seem to be given more varied job positions than anyplace else in the world. Conceivably, as the standard of living improves and there is less economic need by the state and the family for the wife to work, she may find herself for the first time with nothing to do but clean and run a house. Yet discussions with Soviet women indicate that many of them are pleased with their interests outside their family life and will probably seek to continue these activities.

The Russians also have made notable progress in the handling of most of their minority groups. Many groups which were almost entirely illiterate before the revolution have been educated and provided with some measure of responsibility. But despite considerable progress, much remains to be done. It is still possible to find areas in Tashkent, Uzbekistan, which seem no better off than some of the slums of nearby Kabul in Afghanistan. Moreover, those areas which have been forcibly carried into the twentieth century, often bear scars to show how rapid the pace has been. But judging by what we call the "civilized" standards of the West, it is encouraging to see young women working without their veils and their brothers struggling to hasten industrialization. At the very least, the Russians have discarded some of the more blatant aspects of Russification that were a feature of the Czarist governments.

REALITY: *Although conditions in the USSR prior to Stalin's death were often hard to distinguish from those existing in a state of serfdom, since the mid-1950s there have been significant improvements. Concentrating primarily on the economic life, there not only is considerable mobility of labor, but an impressive program of social benefits. Moreover, even on collective farms, real wages have increased steadily in recent years so that even the peasants have been able to purchase a wide range of consumer goods. More and more the consumer seems to be exercising his sovereignty. Those seeking economic conditions comparable to existing Western standards still have a long distance to travel, but at least the Soviet government seems to be moving in that direction.*

CHAPTER 6

MYTH: *The Soviet Union is a land of milk and honey where communism has brought fulfillment and tranquility to everyone.*

Just as there are those who see nothing but evil and retrogression in the Soviet Union, so there are those who see nothing but virtue and progress. Obviously the truth is somewhere in between; exactly where depends on one's political and economic philosophy. In the same way, those who are anti-communist seem to come back from a visit to the USSR feeling that their experiences only justified their hostility, while those who are pro-communist seem to come back equally convinced that everything they saw only verified what they had always thought.

Having directed our debunking to those who see the Soviet Union only as an unrepentant totalitarian superstate, we must now attempt to provide some additional balance for those who think the Soviet Union is an economic paradise on earth. Again, since we are concerned primarily with economic conditions, we have to ignore most of the political shortcomings in the Soviet system. To a certain extent this is impossible because if there is no freedom of expression or movement, economic and industrial life is also affected. In the Soviet Union, the political bureaucracy spreads its frustrating and tension-producing ways into all aspects of existence from which there is little escape. Yet as much as possible we shall restrict our discussion to economic aspects of totalitarianism.

The point to note is that despite the progress that has been made in economic growth, a disproportionate amount of it has been diverted to heavy industry and away from the consumer. We have shown how rapidly conditions have improved for the Soviet citizen in the last few years, but the fact remains that very little was done previously. Of course, this makes the present achievements look much more impressive, but this involves overlooking how bad things were until at least the mid-1950s. In this context, it is depressing to recall that the material standard of living in the early 1950s was no better than it was in the prerevolutionary period. Of course, there had been an improvement in medical care, education, and welfare. But, for consumer goods and housing, this meant there was a 40-year span with no tangible progress in the personal well-being of the people.

No matter how much destruction was suffered by the USSR as a result of the war, it is also necessary to note that many of the European countries such as Holland and Germany suffered as much. The nations of Western Europe of course had the Marshall Plan to boost them ahead. But, then, the Russians had the same opportunity. True it would have meant ideological compromise, but this apparently did not bother the Czechs and Poles who wanted to take part, that is until the Russians insisted that their participation would enslave them to the United States and force them to accept unwanted consumer goods from America's glutted warehouses. More important, the living conditions of the ordinary worker in Western Europe still are much higher than those of the Russian worker.[1] To some extent this is due to the inordinate amount of investment still being diverted to heavy industry in the USSR. Agriculture and light industry, although better regarded than before, are still treated as a poor relation. The distinction in living conditions is especially marked between the USSR and the Scandinavian countries where, in fact, not just in theory, there seem to be no slums.

[1] Stanley Cohn, "Soviet Growth Retardation: Trends in Resource Availability and Efficiency," *New Directions in the Soviet Economy.* Prepared for the Joint Economic Committee, 89th Congress, 2nd session, Washington, D.C., U.S. Government Printing Office, 1966, p. 108.

The ones who have suffered the most in all of this have been the peasants. As noted earlier, Soviet government officials have recently begun to divert resources to the rural areas. They are belatedly recognizing how badly the peasants have been treated. Even now, however, the peasants still tend to be regarded as vestiges of the past that are barely worth conserving. Because some peasants continue to charge exorbitant prices for the fresh commodities they are able to produce in their private plots, many urban residents still think of them as antisocial and unclean and consequently undeserving of even what little help they receive from the state.

We have mentioned that, until recently, there was no provision for pensions for peasants and that most of them received a very low average wage. In the darker days of the 1930s, conditions were much worse. The collective farm was set up with the idea that the peasant would be the risk holder. Thus, theoretically, if there were a bumper crop, the peasants stood to share in a large bounty. Actually, there were several showplace farms that were called *millionaire collectives* because of the constant high returns they earned. The overwhelming majority of farms, however, fared nowhere near as well. In fact, the official prices they received for their crops often failed to cover their costs. No one really knew what the actual costs and prices were. For example, there was no way of determining the cost of labor in advance because the farmer was only entitled to the residual after all expenses had been paid. Similarly, it was hard to evaluate the cost of using a tractor since the Machine Tractor Stations were paid in kind, i.e., they received produce from the farm. But, because there were varying prices for the farm products sold by the collective farm, it was not always clear just how much the Machine Tractor Station was actually receiving in money. There were two official prices. Each farm had a minimal quota it had to deliver, and, for this, they obtained a very low price. If they produced more than this minimal quota, they were entitled to sell the remainder at a higher price. Finally, there was the much higher price that prevailed on the collective farm market. Here the peasants sold produce from their private plots as well as produce from the collective farm which was turned over to the peasants as part of their wage. Prices on the collective farm markets were allowed to form their own level under the relatively unhampered influence of supply and demand.

Looking back on the period, many Soviet economists argue that grain production did not grow because the prevailing price system for the required deliveries actually penalized the farmer. Because prices were held so low, many peasants felt that the more they produced the worse off they were, since their quotas would always be increased. This was not all unintentional. Stalin had designed the collective farms so that they not only stood to benefit from the bounty that was somehow always just over the horizon, but they also stood to share the loss. If there was a drought or a bad growing season, this was the peasants' burden to bear. There was no such thing as a program of farm subsidies. In fact, there seemed to be just the opposite. Franklyn D. Holzman shows that the Soviet government imposed a tax of about 70 to 80 per cent on the price of bread.[2] This was one of the highest tax rates that existed in the USSR. It was an extremely regressive tax, something that one would not ordinarily expect in a communist country. Part of the burden was carried by the farmer who received less than his costs on a portion of his product, and the rest was paid by the consumer who had to pay a considerable markup over what the farmer received. Conditions improved significantly in the 1950s when the procurement price paid the peasant rose, Khrushchev abolished the Machine Tractor Stations, and the state invested more money in agriculture. But, for too many years, the agricultural sector was made to bear an onerous burden.

To the extent that the peasants had to depend on the collective farms for their income, they lived on the far fringe of economic survival. Inevitably, most of them preferred to spend their time on their private plots of land. Each peasant was allocated about one-half hectare, usually adjacent to his home, where he could grow what he pleased. Most peasants chose to grow fruits and vegetables, which always seemed to be in short supply except at the very height of the growing season. They could also raise a limited amount of livestock. Because of the shortage of such products, the peasants were able to earn very high prices for their private efforts, more in fact than they earned from their work on the collective farm itself. In turn, this

[2] Franklyn D. Holzman, *Soviet Taxation*. Cambridge, Mass.: Harvard University Press, 1955, p. 153.

caused resentment among urban residents, and it also caused the peasants to underfulfill their work assignments in the collective sector. Finally this lowered the production of the collective farms.

The abuse by the state of the peasant extended beyond the fact that he was underpaid for his efforts. In the worst tradition of the "company store," the peasants were also taken advantage of whenever they bought anything for their personal use. Because of the state monopoly over all retail trade, except the collective farm markets, the government was able to decree what facilities should be made available in the rural areas. In line with the cooperative spirit that was supposed to govern life on the collective farm, the government decided to create a network of cooperative stores in the countryside. These cooperative stores were given monopoly rights over all retail trade. A similar monopoly was created in the urban areas by the government store network.

Within a short time, it became clear that the cooperative stores were to be as cooperative in their operations as the collective farms. If something is called a cooperative store, the normal assumption is that it will be run like a cooperative found anyplace else in the world. This should mean that prices are comparable to those in non-competitive stores and that members should receive a rebate commensurate with the size of their purchase and the sales volume of the store. As we have discovered, however, logic can be a fragile guide in the Soviet Union. In fact, until 1966, prices in the cooperative store were 7 per cent higher than comparable prices in the urban network of government stores. There had been an equalization of some prices prior to 1966, but it was only in January of that year that complete parity was decreed. Moreover, there is little to indicate that the payment of rebates was a regular procedure. In a word, the peasants were paying for it coming and going.

Under the circumstances, it was only to be expected that retail sales volume in the rural villages was considerably less than in the urban centers. Despite the fact that there were more people in the countryside than there were in the cities until after World War II, retail sales in the countryside often amounted to less than 25 per cent of what was sold in urban areas and apparently never totaled more than 30 per cent. This was a reflection not only of the disparity in prices but also the poorer quality of merchandise that was sent to the

66

rural areas. Moreover, the stores themselves were often neglected and inferior to urban facilities. Similar disparities seem to exist all over the world. Rural trade facilities often leave much to be desired. In the Soviet Union, it was official state policy from which there was no appeal.

Checks and Balances

The difficulty of seeking an appeal against a government policy illustrates another problem that exists in a society in which the state exercises monopoly control over the economy. Most of us have heard stories enough about petty government tyrants (they need not be in the government; they can be in any kind of bureaucracy, even the university) in the United States and Western Europe who seem unable to respond to an immediate problem with any kind of compassion. Occasionally a more sympathetic bureaucrat will explain feebly that he would like to help, but the rules will not let him. The Soviet Union has more than its share of sympathetic and not so sympathetic officials in charge of normal state activities. But remember, in addition to the regular complement of such officials, it is the Soviet government that also monopolizes all aspects of the economy. In effect, therefore, there is no court of appeal on government policy outside of the government itself.

One of the unappreciated beauties of the American system is that a person can usually find alternative sources of support when he finds himself at odds with the prevailing values of the system. Normally, if someone is excluded from government work because of his views, it is not too hard to find alternative employment in private industry. And as some critics of our government charge, there are even instances when those who are unable to hold a job in private industry find employment with the government. During the McCarthy period in the United States, it sometimes was hard for writers and entertainers to find work in their fields, but those who were forced to forsake their profession were normally able to find alternative, if not commensurate, work. This was not always a pleasant situation. Nonetheless, I knew of a Marxist instructor of history who was fired by his college and took a job, instead, as a manager of an electronics factory.

As unfortunate or fortunate as such stories are in this or other Western countries, they usually do not have nearly as happy endings in the USSR. If one is put on a Soviet blacklist, he cannot escape the government by finding work (even manual labor) in private industry. There is no private industry. Like it or not, the citizen must face a government official wherever he works. This can be an effective device for channeling dissent. As we indicated earlier, the writer Alexander Solzhenitsyn apparently has tangled with just such a bureaucratic blockade.

The government's control over all economic resources affects, not only the individual's desire to dissent, but his ability to convey that protest. Even though what Solzhenitsyn was saying did not threaten the existence of the state, he was not allowed to communicate his ideas to others.[3] In much the same way, similar obstacles confront any Soviet citizen who might want to challenge a particular policy of the state.

All states have the power to tax. But usually the power to tax is restricted so that state officials cannot destroy those with whom it disagrees. Soviet control over economic power, however, goes far beyond the power of taxation. The state in the USSR has the power to destroy any independent economic power base. It is illegal for an individual citizen or group of citizens to build up an economic power base in the USSR. There are occasions when such power bases are built up illegally, but as soon as they are discovered, they are destroyed. Anyone who criticizes the state or its policies risks the loss of his economic livelihood.

One of the features of the economic systems in the Western world is the relative ease with which people can form their own economic power bases. Even if there is some dispute whether it is as easy to accumulate an independent base as it once was, it still happens every day. Of course it does not always follow that economic independence leads to political dissent. If anything, economic independence usually engenders satisfaction with the status quo and support of existing government policies. But there are important exceptions. In fact, most

[3] *Survey,* July, 1967, p. 177.

revolutions that have taken place in the last few centuries were led by members of the middle class whose economic positions were secure enough to sustain them through any economic pressure. At the same time, it is not necessary to have a middle class in order to have economic independence. Poorer members of society may deem it in their interest to contribute their funds to groups which support their views, but, again, the important thing is that such groups must be allowed to maintain an existence of their own, independent of the state. They can then buy a duplicating machine or conceivably hire a printing press to disseminate their ideas. Presumably, if the ideas and pleas strike a responsive note, the protest groups will be able to attract an even larger following. The formation of such independent groups in the USSR is against the law. All groups are supposed to fit within the general framework of officially sponsored organizations. Moreover, access to duplicating equipment is closely regulated. Those who want to circulate anything through unauthorized channels must usually fall back on carbon paper. Communist officials have been so sensitive about the possibility of clandestine publications that, during the 1950s, they used to lock up all state-owned duplicating equipment during official holidays. Complete control was then assumed because no one was permitted the private ownership of such equipment. Nonetheless, despite such controls, private manuscripts have been circulated hand to hand, increasingly so after the death of Stalin.

Trade Unions

The Soviet Union has acted to see that every group is included somewhere in the state structure. It is only natural, therefore, that organizations like the trade unions which usually serve as a channel of protest should be restricted to serve the interests of the state. All trade unions are directly controlled and are considered part of the governing apparatus of the state. There is therefore usually no way for the workers to unite in protest against improper working conditions in state-owned factories except through state-run unions. Because his job is dependent on state approval rather than worker approval, the trade union official generally finds his position little different from that of the factory worker. Both try to satisfy their employer, which is the state. By contrast, it often happens in Western societies that the union leader is beholden only to the factory workers. This means his performance is measured by the success he has in opposing the interests of the manufacturing authorities. On occasion, this has even involved violence. Normally, however, the long-run interests of both sides in the West are served by peaceful but meaningful negotiations. The important point, however, is that the union representative is not dependent financially on the directors of the factory. Therefore, he runs no economic risk in opposing them. Thus, Western labor union leaders are expected to defend workers' rights and seek higher pay through collective bargaining. In the Soviet Union, however, the state cannot tolerate a strike against itself or a rise in wages beyond what it, as client and judge, determines is appropriate. There is therefore no meaningful collective bargaining, and strikes are illegal. Of course, the size of a worker's wage in the West is not dependent solely on an actual strike by his union, but the ability to strike is a very potent persuader. The Soviet worker lacks this right.

Oddly enough, despite the emasculation of the unions' role on the basic question of workers' rights, there have been strikes. Such strikes are not authorized nor are they usually led by union officials. Yet, when work conditions are bad enough, Soviet workers have been known to form together in almost spontaneous fashion and walk off their jobs. Naturally, strikes in the Soviet Union are not a common occurrence. They are usually precipitated by an increase in work norms with little or no increase in compensation. Settlement is usually reached by the reduction of the norms and the replacement of the factory manager. On occasion, however, troops have had to be called, as at Novocherkassk near Rostow in 1962.[4] That workers who are prevented from seeking redress for their grievances or bargaining collectively within an institutionalized framework must resort to such an extreme form of protest indicates how serious such conditions can become. This is something that the more outspoken supporters of the Soviet system often fail to see or acknowledge.

In other less important areas, the Soviet trade unions do have some

[4] Emily Clark Brown, *Soviet Trade Unions and Labor Relations.* Cambridge, Mass.: Harvard University Press, 1966, p. 235.

positive role to play. They have responsibility for a large portion of the welfare activities conducted within the country. The trade unions run many of the resort areas and children's camps. Unions also play a very important part in acculturating the peasants to the industrial life of the urban centers. By providing additional schooling, they have also helped to upgrade the skills of their members. Nonetheless, this can hardly be described as strident unionism. In fact, Soviet unions generally have served more to push up worker's norms and production targets than they have sought to reduce them.

The Party and Favoritism

Without free and independent trade unions, it is conceivable but most unlikely that a country will be democratic. The trade unions usually serve as a rallying point against those in control. Nonetheless, in lieu of an effective trade union system, it might be possible for a political party to watch over the interests of those at the bottom of the production line. Unfortunately there is no party of protest in the USSR. In many countries of the world, it is frequently the Communist Party which serves as an important vehicle, even if an extreme one, for dissent and opposition. But, in the Soviet Union the Party represents the vested interests and there is no other party. Most of the members of the Soviet Communist Party are from the upper and middle classes of society. They are the order givers, i.e., the managers, the foremen, and the mayors. In fact, ability and power are usually prerequisites for party membership. Thus, today, there are few members of the unskilled proletariat who are even eligible for membership. This means there is no one these people can turn to for support to defend their interests against the manager, the foreman, or the mayor.

At the same time that there are some in the USSR who want to protest but find themselves limited as to what they can do, others in Soviet society find that there is virtually no restraint on their activity. As we have seen, the absence of private enterprise removes one of the links in the usual checks-and-balances system. Since there is no effective body of opposition outside the Communist Party, there is one less check on abuses in the economic system. Consequently, anyone at an upper level of the Party can only be scrutinized by someone at even a higher level of the Party. Of course, there are control commissions and inspectorates within the Party or government which are supposed to ensure that there are no abuses; but these groups are still linked to the people and Party in control. In any case, these commissions must report to senior officials in the line of command before any corrective measures will be taken. Very often so-called "family circles" develop between the local officials and the inspectors. The basis of this association is essentially "you scratch my back and I'll scratch yours"; one official protects his comrade, his comrade protects him, and both of them do more or less as they please.[5] Occasionally lower level citizens make their feelings known through letters to the newspapers and senior officials, but this always subjects the complainer to the danger of punitive action. Except for such indirect methods, there is no built-in system outside the official Party or government.

Therefore, guided only by their own consciences, many Soviet officials openly abuse the system. Even the most conscientious official finds it hard to resist seeking some extra favor for his children. This may take the form of requesting a little help in securing admission to the right school or university or obtaining the right kind of job in the right city. No matter how pristine his revolutionary fervor, every parent finds himself subject to such temptations. Once such favors are sought, however, the official is compromised. Subsequently, he finds it less difficult to seek other favors and privileges.

A subsidiary aspect of such favor seeking is that social and economic mobility in the system is adversely affected. By having a father or mother who is well placed in the bureaucracy of either the Party or government, a child is more likely to rise to the top than is his peer whose parents are not so influential. Stalin's son Vasily showed what a person could do when it was thought he had the protection of the highest authorities. Despite playboy-like debaucheries and lack of experience, Vasily was made a Lieutenant General at the tender age of 24. Yet, there still is an impressive amount of mobility in the USSR because new positions and new specialties continue to open up rapidly. Unquestionably, however, there is less mobility now than there was in the 1920s, 1930s, and 1940s. Mobility was ex-

[5] Joseph S. Berliner, *Factory and Manager in the USSR*. Cambridge, Mass.: Harvard University Press, 1957, pp. 259-263.

ceptionally rapid then because of the purges and the war. But even more important was the fact that the rapid expansion of industry and government created an immense need for numerous specialists and officials. This meant opportunities were virtually unlimited. But, once these positions were filled with young people and the rate of expansion had begun to taper off, the job opportunities were no longer as plentiful. People who were in their thirties in the 1930s are only now beginning to retire. With fewer job vacancies, there are fewer individuals who will be able to make it to the top. Consequently when there are two people with equal talent, and sometimes with unequal talent, the one with a little extra influence is more likely to succeed. It would be worthwhile if someone would study the subject in greater detail, but from what is known about the children and children-in-law of senior Soviet officials, most of them appear to have comfortable jobs in important government offices, universities, or research institutes. There have been few, if any, instances where the child of an important official has found it necessary to take a subordinate position in a factory.[6] As long as a Soviet official is not purged, his relatives remain well-protected. It would be too much to say that this was a totalitarian aspect of Soviet society since it seems common to almost every society in the world. Nonetheless, in other countries when nepotism proves to be an obstacle in government organizations, there is always the private sector. And when there is nepotism in the private sector which may block advancement for someone who is not the boss's son, there is always the public sector. Again, the monopolization by the government in the Soviet Union of both sectors eliminates an important alternative.

Minorities

In the last chapter we saw how well minority groups were treated. Now it is necessary to look at the other side of the story. Like so much else in the Soviet Union, the Soviet policy toward minority groups is better in theory than it is in practice. The Great Russians, the domi-

[6] Alex Inkeles, "Social Stratification and Mobility in the Soviet Union: 1940-1950," *American Sociological Review,* 15, No. 4 (August, 1950), 465-479.

nant group in the Soviet Union, tend to be very chauvinistic and deprecatory of the abilities and contributions of other national and social groups. Peoples from the Caucasus are thought of as schemers, and peoples from Central Asia as inert. The White Russians and the Ukrainians are considered more able than the Asians and the Trans-caucasians but, of course, less able than the Great Russians. All of them distrust the Jews.

Naturally the minorities reciprocate the feelings of the Russians. They know how the Russians feel and they can never quite forget the policy of Russification that was so important in prerevolutionary times. As indicated in the previous chapter, they concede that there has been considerable improvement in the official attitude toward nationality groups within the USSR, but they feel there is still a long way to go. A manifestation of these difficulties is indicated by the fights between Russian and Uzbeck groups of children in Tashkent. While the city is becoming more and more integrated and the Uzbecks are obtaining better and better jobs, the poorer housing districts are almost all Uzbeck. Furthermore, it would be most unusual to find a Russian in Tashkent with a menial job.

There is a broader economic aspect to the nationality problem. It is difficult, if not impossible, to prove, but many of the nationality groups, especially the Central Asians, insist that there has been a net outflow of resources from their republics and territorial regions to Great Russia, and to Moscow in particular. The one major exception to this is Georgia, which apparently received special treatment from Stalin who himself was a Georgian. In their more dramatic and per-haps exaggerated moments, several minority groups have likened their economic conditions to the vassal states of old which periodically sent tribute to the feudal center. No one denies that Moscow has sent large quantities of capital to build up the economies of these provincial areas. All they argue is that whatever Moscow sends in has been well paid for by previous economic extractions.[7]

[7] In a sense, such feelings are reminiscent of the bitterness of midwesterners and westerners in the nineteenth century toward Wall Street. There was intense resentment over what appeared to be the flow of material wealth to the East Coast in exchange for a meager investment.

Before leaving this section, it is necessary to add something more about the effect of a bureaucracy in the balance between totalitarian and democratic forms of government. We have already discussed the consequences of the absence of a system of checks and balances in the Soviet economic system. Bureaucracy is cumbersome enough under any system or in any organization, but it is particularly bothersome when there appears to be little control over or alternative to it. More important, it is necessary to understand that the bureaucrat controls almost all decision making in the USSR. This is an all-important consideration in an industrialized society.

Because a society calls itself communist or socialist, there is no reason to assume that functional relationships within the society have changed. The nature of an industrialized society, in fact, virtually precludes much in the way of a radical change. Machines must be operated at certain times and places, and resources must be moved back and forth according to prearranged schedules. People, machinery, and material must all be interrelated, and someone has to decide when and where such interrelationships are to take place. This means someone within the system has the right to hire and fire. Conceivably the trade union could step in as a buffer, and sometimes it does. However, because both the union and the factory are organs of the state, there are many occasions when there is inadequate protection for the individual factory worker against the factory manager. The farm manager has the same degree of power over the peasants.

For the individual, the big question remains: What control does he have over his own destiny? The point being made here is that such concerns do not vanish for the worker in the industrialized state just because someone comes along and says that tomorrow he will be living in a communist society. Whether he is in a capitalist or a communist state, the average worker still is intimidated by any superior who has the power of economic life or death over him. Even if this power is not abused, the subordinate will still find himself ordered to perform tasks that do not necessarily appeal to him. Someone must still work the night shift, someone must still go into the coal mines, and someone must still wash the dishes and collect the garbage. There can be no other way in the industrialized state. Coordination of all the parts is an absolute necessity, and positions of responsibility must be created to make sure that the member parts function properly and that all the necessary work is done by someone. To make this possible, those who refuse to fulfill their obligations must be penalized with lower pay or dismissal. Consequently, regardless of ideology, it seems inevitable in any industrialized state that there must be some who give and some who take orders and that there be some who must have decision-making power over others. The Soviet Union is no exception.

REALITY: *Although the Soviet Union is not an earthly hell, neither is it a heaven on earth. Many aspects of the despotic past remain. Moreover, because the operation of the state and the economy are combined, the checks and balances which existed between the two sectors in other countries have been destroyed in the USSR. This eliminates an important set of options for the individual within the state. Finally, changing the description of an economic system does nothing to end the domination of one man by another. All industrialized societies are structured so that orders must be issued by one group and accepted by others. As long as this process continues, there must always be someone who will have to do the dirty work, and there will probably be those who will object to being ordered about, no matter what they are doing.*

PART III

Operation
of the Economy

MYTH: *The Soviet economic system is inefficient and irrational. There is little sophistication or innovation.*

Having considered some of the political-economic myths about the Soviet Union, it is time to examine how the Soviet economy operates. Inevitably many legends have arisen about the ineffectiveness of the Soviet economy. It should not surprise us if we find many of them are contradictory.

The best rebuttal to those who insist that the Soviet economy is nothing but chaos and confusion is to show how rapidly the Soviet economy has grown in the last 50 years. As we have indicated, other countries may have done as well, and the Soviet Union might have done even better if it had avoided the waste and destruction of the civil war and the collectivization period, but whatever the alternatives, the Russians have become the world's second largest industrial power. If anything, their heavy industrial sector is overdeveloped. Despite the problems the Russians may currently be having, even Western economists agree that Russia's GNP has increased every year since World War II and that its rate of economic growth has recently regained a little of its previous momentum.

With such a solid industrial structure, it stands to reason that the Russians have also been able to produce some sophisticated equipment. To anyone who has followed their space exploits, this is clear. As the years go by, it becomes more difficult to recapture the panic that prevailed in the West when the Russians sent the world's first sputnik skyward in 1957. Yuri Gagarin's manned flight a few years later did nothing to dispel this hysteria. Comparable American space achievements lagged two or three years behind for what seemed to be a depressingly long period of time. Throughout that period, it became clear to all but the most dogmatic skeptics that the Russians had attained an impressive mastery over science and technology. Much the same type of mastery was necessary before they could develop their atomic and hydrogen bombs. But in the Soviet space triumph, no one could say, as was said of their work on the bombs, that the Russians had stolen all their information from us. In 1957, we had more to steal from the Russians than they had to steal from us.

No matter how it was rationalized, it was clear that the Russians had developed new materials, new fuels, new electronic equipment, and new space skills that were superior to anything else then produced. Moreover, Soviet industry had taken ideas and transformed them into the finished space ship. It could no longer be argued that the Soviet economy was incapable of innovating on its own.

As foreign observers began to look more closely at Soviet accomplishments, they saw that Soviet achievements extended far beyond the realm of space technology. For example, the Russians had developed a whole fleet of hydrofoil riverboats. Although experimental ships had been designed by Westerners during the 1940s, nothing had come of it. In contrast, the Russians were using their hydrofoils on regularly scheduled runs along all their main inland waterways for passengers and freight. They have even begun to sell hydrofoil craft to other countries. In the same way, the Russian aircraft industry has developed an impressive variety of aircraft. Their civil and military aircraft have always been regarded with respect in the West. They have also made powerful strides in the development of helicopters and vertical-lift airplanes (VTOL). There are reports that they have also made rapid progress in the manufacture of a supersonic transport and, indeed, are ahead of the United States in the development of this plane.

The Russians have also mastered some of the more traditional industrial processes. To some, the older sections of Moscow's subway system may seem excessively ornate, but most observers agree that the subways in Moscow and Leningrad are among the most efficient and comfortable in the world. The Russians also lead the world in many phases of ferrous metallurgy. A delegation from the American Iron and Steel Institute found in 1959 that the Russian blast furnaces were yielding double the output of comparable American blast furnaces. In their electric steel furnaces they were able to extract almost 50 per cent more than metallurgists in the United States.[1] In recent years the Russians have gone on to build still bigger and better blast furnaces and open hearth furnaces.

The Russians have also gone on to outproduce the United States in the extraction of coal and iron ore, and the production of such products as railroad locomotives, cement, woolen fabrics, and refined sugar. Reflecting the same drive, the Russians have become the world's second largest exporter of watches, surpassed only by the Swiss. Their success in the watch industry is especially satisfying to the Russians since, prior to World War II, only a few thousand watches a year were produced in the whole country. In fact, one reason the Russians acquired the image of such an industrially backward country was that the goal of every Russian soldier in Europe at the end of World War II was to take home a watch. Even though many foreigners still think of the Russians in this context, Soviet watches now flood the markets of Africa and Asia and are making inroads into Swiss markets in Europe.

Because they own and control all economic activity in the country, the Russians have been able to create entirely new organizational forms of activity in some industries. Because of the uniqueness of their situation, the Russians are able to take advantage of the economies of scale in a way that would be impossible in most other countries. For example, the fishing industry in other countries of the world consists of independent fishermen who own and sometimes operate their own boats. Occasionally one firm may control several boats, but generally there are no large-scale operations. By contrast, in the USSR the state owns all the boats and is in a position to coordinate all fishing activities. Recognizing the potential in such a situation, the Ministry of Fishing decided to set up a system of mobile fishing fleets in which groups of fishing trawlers were assigned to larger mother ships. These mother ships have been designed to serve as

[1] M. Gardner Clark, "Economics and Technology: The Case of Soviet Steel," *Study of the Soviet Economy*, Nicolas Spulber, ed. The Hague: Morton and Company, 1961, pp. 22-23.

supplying and receiving vessels. This made it possible for the smaller Soviet trawlers to remain away from port for long periods of time. Instead of returning to port every time they filled their nets, the trawlers were able to unload their fish on the mother ship, which processes the catch at sea. With such a system, the trawlers have been able to spend more time trawling and less time traveling back and forth to port. Because of this arrangement, the Russians have been able to invade foreign fishing preserves at will. At times, they even outnumber the American fishermen at Georges Banks directly off the American east coast. Such a system of fishing seems to be possible only when there is common ownership over a sufficiently large number of boats.

Almost the same potential existed in the construction industry. Whereas the construction industry in most countries is made up of many small contractors, in the Soviet Union the state does all the construction work. In effect, the work in the USSR has been performed by a variety of contracting enterprises, but they were all owned by the state. While Khrushchev was in power, he saw the advantage of trying to introduce mass production techniques in building construction. Normally the field is dominated by small craftsmen who build to order and therefore are unable to produce in large quantities. Khrushchev was an enthusiastic supporter of the idea that all housing should be standardized and built according to a general plan. This made it possible to prefabricate most of the parts in advance. By producing component parts at factory sites and transporting them in large trucks to the building site, Khrushchev reasoned that buildings could be constructed more cheaply and quickly than if everything were built on the site. Apartment buildings and factories are now built this way all over the Soviet Union. We saw in Chapter 4 how this system made possible the rapid increase in apartment construction.

There are undoubtedly clear advantages to such a system. Where possible, American manufacturers have also tried to use more pre-assembled components. As an example, few contractors today mix their own cement; most of them have it delivered in premixed form from huge tank trucks. Similarly, window and door frames come assembled and ready for installation. Some of our larger contractors have even tried their hand at building prefabricated homes in the often homogeneous housing projects that fill our suburbs. The Levit-

82

town projects are a good example. Such standardization makes it possible to build a home for a much lower price.

But just as there are advantages to prefabrication in construction, so there are disadvantages. As is apparent to anyone who has seen an American housing project, there is usually little if any variety. Fortunately, in the United States, there are numerous contractors building numerous projects. As a result, there is at least some variety among projects. Because there are fewer contractors and because the work is coordinated by the state in the USSR, there is less variety. The monotony in fact is depressing.

Saving and Investing

Although it meant neglecting the consumer, the Soviet system turned out to be an ideal instrument for extracting savings and turning them into capital investment. In most societies, savings and investment are a function of the interest rate and individual reactions to the opportunities that present themselves. Economists generally agree that one of their most difficult problems in economic development is to convince individuals and private units that they should abstain from consumption. Since such groups in an underdeveloped country are often poor to begin with, there is not much room for further abstention. If by some means saving is induced, the next and equally difficult task is to direct these savings into productive and long-term investment. Because of their country's and their own insecurity, those who do save in an undeveloped country are reluctant to commit their money for any long-term projects. Everyone wants to earn an immediate return on his money so it can be withdrawn quickly. Few savers or investors in these circumstances have what economists call long "time horizons." They can only see two or three years ahead, and this is not a lengthy enough period for economic development.

By contrast, after the renationalization of all industry at the end of the NEP period, the Russians found that their problem was much simpler. Since they had decreed that all productive property was theirs, they could direct investment into whatever areas they selected.

Furthermore, they tended to select projects with exceptionally long periods of maturation. This was why the Russians were able to undertake such projects as the Dnepropetrovsk, Kuibyshev, and Bratsk dams. For much the same reason, Stalin was able to build his subways and pursue his dream to make the Volga and Don Rivers a link between the Black Sea and Moscow. As we shall see, if anything, the time horizon of Stalin and his successors was too long. This meant that the fruits of their investment could not be enjoyed for many years, and consequently consumption was considerably less than had been anticipated.

One of the advantages and at the same time one of the disadvantages of this kind of system is that there may be very weak or no restraint on the government to limit the amount of saving that is demanded. Because the state owns everything, the planning officials do not have to worry about what the interest rate must be to induce the desired amount of saving. The state can generate almost any saving it wants simply by paying low *real* salaries. It can pay high money salaries and either tax away large sums or inflate away what it wants by failing to put enough goods on the shelf and by charging high prices for those it does sell. This clearly is a valuable tool for any group that wants to expand rapidly. Unfortunately, the majority of the population may wish to grow at a slower rate and enjoy more consumption in the present since they may never live to see what is called "the future." But there is usually little these people can do to protest the decisions of the central planners. After Stalin's death, most of the East European governments confessed that there had indeed been too much enthusiasm by the planners in their countries and that the planners had completely neglected the needs of their populations prior to 1953. Because they are much less candid about their problems, the Russians have had somewhat less to say publicly about the matter. Nonetheless, by implication, they were guilty of the same oversaving.

Although such calculations are subject to statistical imprecision, Western scholars have estimated that annual Gross Fixed Capital Formation as a per cent of Gross Domestic Product in the USSR was about 24 per cent.[2] This is a fairly high level. By contrast, the similar

[2] Abram Bergson and Simon Kuznets, eds., *Economic Trends in the Soviet Union.* Cambridge, Mass.: Harvard University Press, 1963, p. 355.

ratio in the United States from 1950 to 1959 was 16.5 per cent. This explains both the massive project building in the USSR and the relatively backward level of personal consumption.

We have concentrated here and in the earlier chapters on only a few of the advantages in the Soviet economic system. Obviously there are many more, but no matter how many disadvantages are cited to offset them, it still must be acknowledged that the Soviet economy is an impressive engine of growth.

REALITY: *The economic system in the USSR is not perfect, but neither is it chaotic. There has been substantial growth as well as sizable innovation. The most convincing testimony to the efficiency of the Soviet economy is the fact that it has grown as rapidly as it has.*

CHAPTER 8

MYTH: *The Soviet economic system is an agile giant that is outclassing and surpassing all known economic systems. Because the state owns all the tools of production, the Soviet Union is able to avoid wasteful competition among private manufacturers. As a result, innovation and flexibility are encouraged and the Soviet Union leads the world in industrial technology and sophistication.*

Like almost everything else concerned with the Soviet Union, one man's myth is often another man's reality. In this case, those who feel the Russians are absolutely incompetent when it comes to economic efficiency are countered by those who feel the Russians can do no wrong. Since we have discussed how the Russians can indeed do well, it is now necessary to show that they do not always do all that well.

The first thing to note is that there are limitations to the advantages that come from putting all control over economic resources in the hands of a single governmental agency. The economies of scale that we noted in the fish ministry and the housing industry do not necessarily extend to all industrial activities. After a time, it even appears that economies of operating scale are more than offset by diseconomies of administration. As enterprises grow in size, it becomes ever more difficult to maintain communications with the outlying parts. Even if communications can be extended, there must be ever-broadening pyramids erected to process and digest the quantity of raw data that filters through.[1] Finally, there must be wider and wider administrative extensions to supervise all the underlying activity. This leads to bureaucracy.

It must also be pointed out that the economies of scale that are so attractive in the USSR are not dependent on complete government ownership of all economic resources in the country. The size of the market and the availability of capital may be of equal or greater importance in determining whether there will be economies of scale. For example, the eventual flourishing of the "piggyback" concept in transportation required that entrepreneurs have vision and capital enough to service the trucking, the railroad, and ultimately the shipping industry. It is true that the government initially encouraged the use of piggyback freight in ocean shipping and could easily have financed the spread of such service to all forms of transportation. But in an economy the size of the United States, there were also many private sources that were able to finance an extensive project of this sort. Even more important, the stimulus for the piggyback system in all forms of transportation came from private industry. Consequently, in order to succeed, it is necessary to have not only capital and control but also ideas and entrepreneurial push.

Innovation

Although Soviet officials have discovered how to monopolize capital and control in the hands of the state, they have not found a way to ensure that the state economic authorities have a similar monopoly on ideas or, more important, on the best ideas. Moreover, even those ideas that originate in the state sector do not always work their way through the bureaucratic mazes that governments tend to create. As long as the government exercises monopoly control over capital and other economic resources, there is usually no alternative when the government rejects a project. At best, an inventor may be able to appeal to a superior official somewhere higher in the chain of com-

[1] Leon Smolinski, "What Next in Soviet Planning," *Foreign Affairs*, July, 1964, p. 602.

mand. But, as is so depressingly illustrated in the Soviet novel *Not By Bread Alone by* V. Dudentsev, there is normally no alternative when a government official vetoes a project. Certainly some vetoes may be deserved. Many good ideas, however, will never even be given a chance to prove their worth as long as there is no court of appeal from a government veto over capital and resources.

Although the right decision by a government planner can bring about impressive growth, the wrong decision can lead to disaster. Once a decision is taken in the Soviet Union, there is a tendency to concentrate all the resources of the state on that particular objective. Usually, no exceptions are tolerated since exceptions make for sloppiness and state planners thrive on order and neatness. The planner tends to be very cautious because he knows that, if a mistake is made, there are usually no alternative plans to fall back on. Speculation or extreme solutions are therefore discouraged because the consequences for the whole economy may be so enormous.

In private enterprise, there are more variations and, therefore, it is less likely that the economy will find itself in an all or nothing situation. While there are many who will seek the conservative middle ground, there are others who will be free to speculate and try the wild venture. This means there will be many failures, but the society as a whole will not suffer unduly because there will always be some who take the safe and sure approach. Most important, there will be others, usually in smaller firms, who will take the big risk and put everything they have on coming out a big winner. This means there will probably be more innovation and there is a greater likelihood of a major breakthrough. Of course, if the private entrepreneurs miscalculate and do exactly the wrong thing, like the Tucker Automobile Company, we may never hear of them again. If they are successful, they may turn into Polaroids or Xeroxes. With state ownership over all the resources, there is no such range of opportunities open to the Russians.

For many years the lack of leadership in innovation did not cause much insomnia among Soviet leaders. The Russians were struggling so valiantly to catch up that they had little time to worry about moving ahead. Consequently, they were content to let foreigners innovate and then to copy from them. In fact, this made it possible for them to avoid all the anguish and cost that accompanied the original research and development; instead, they could pick the fruits of someone else's labor and frustration. Up to a certain point, such policies helped them to narrow the gap between the more innovative economies and their own.

Western manufacturers found themselves facing competition, in some cases, from adaptions of their own equipment which had been produced in the USSR. Foreign companies such as Ford were occasionally paid to build factories for the Russians; but, with increasing frequency, the Russians simply bought a few prototype models and then set out to produce their own variations with no acknowledgment. Since the Russians did not fully adhere to international patent agreements, this created hesitancy among foreign manufacturers when they received orders for a few selected models from the Russians. Such a policy nevertheless helped Russia catch up rapidly at relatively little cost.

Although imitative adaption was generally easier than original exploration, the Russians did not completely avoid the challenge of innovation. Because of limited talent and other resources, they chose to concentrate their innovative efforts in certain priority areas. For the most part, this meant they devoted themselves to military technology. This was later extended to atomic and space research and production.

Occasionally, some technological bottleneck might arise that was unique to the USSR. In such a situation, they were usually unable to find anything to copy from the West and consequently were forced to include such problems in their priority research. For example, because their workmanship was sloppy, the Russians were unable to produce drillpipe that was of high enough quality to withstand the pressures generated in oil drilling. Consequently, they were forced to devise a whole new approach, which resulted in the development of the turbodrill.[2]

Because of such accomplishments, the whole world soon came to appreciate their abilities and was impressed with their often spectacular achievements. By analogy, it was generally assumed that, if the Russians were so able in some fields, they must be equally able in other fields; but this was not so. It became clear with time that the

[2] Robert W. Campbell, *Soviet Economic Power,* 2nd ed. Boston: Houghton-Mifflin, 1966, p. 60.

Russians were able to make as much progress as they did only because they neglected everything else. They took their best engineers and their best craftsmen and set them to work on a limited set of problems. This policy paid off in several impressive successes, but it necessitated the neglect of product innovation in a large part of the rest of the economy.

The Planning System

Given the heavily centralized nature of the planning system and the type of incentives arrangement which existed until 1965, it was only natural that plant managers would display little innovation and initiative. Enterprise targets were always derived from the yearly and Five-Year Plans that were set in Moscow. Just as the annual plans were set in some quantitative terms such as 80 million tons of cement, 2 million nails, or 5 million square meters of cotton cloth, so the industrial factory was assigned some target spelled out in physical terms. Called the *val* system, this output target served as the main measure of managerial success. If a factory managed to produce its quota of whatever it was producing, the factory manager was judged to be a good one and he and his workers were awarded a bonus. If he exceeded the quota, he was praised as an excellent manager and he and his workers were presented an even higher bonus. In contrast, underfulfillment of the plan, even by 1 per cent, meant the manager would not receive his full salary; thus the manager always made an intensive effort to push that extra distance and quantity for the bonus.

Although *val* was the main success criterion for the manager, there were several other targets as well.[3] If he could, the manager was supposed to observe the targets that were set on such things as labor productivity, number of workers, wages, capital investment, production costs, and profit. But all such quotas were subordinate to the output target. Consequently, *val* came first. Fulfillment of the labor productivity or profit target was a nice thing for the manager to boast

[3] For a thorough discussion of success indicators, see Alec Nove, *The Soviet Economy: An Introduction*, New York: Praeger, 1962, p. 155.

about, but it did not mean a thing unless the output was also fulfilled.

With such a system, the manager and his work force devoted all their efforts to fulfillment of their particular output target. If, along the way, it was possible to meet some other assigned target, so much the better; if not, no one seemed to care. This inevitably meant that costs of production and profitable operation were frequently sacrificed to reach the output goal. Since the manager's pay check depended on meeting his output target, he was not especially concerned if he did not use his supplies economically. He was not penalized for waste; he was penalized for underfulfillment of output. Russian planners ultimately came to realize the folly of such a system and ordered that production costs would also have to be fulfilled in order to qualify for bonuses. Unfortunately, this change brought only slight improvement, and *val* remained the main determinant of bonuses until 1965.

Soviet factory managers soon discovered there were many ways in which they could fulfill their quotas and qualify for a premium. The easiest way to avoid ulcers was to lobby for a low target. Obviously, the lower the target, the easier it would be to fulfill it. Inevitably, there were always complaints that managers were spending more time on fighting for easy targets than on fulfilling the plan. In a real sense, success as a manager was just as dependent on bargaining skill as on productive ability. At the same time, the manager soon realized that, if he overfulfilled his targets with too much ease, the supervising planning authorities would increase the targets in the next period. The end result was that the manager held back his productive abilities and reserves for fear that he would be penalized in the future.

A by-product of the system of planned targets was that each manager tried to become self-sufficient. It was bad enough when there were production problems within his own factory; for that, the manager was prepared to lose his bonus. But it was intolerable when a manager found that he could not fulfill his quota because his suppliers had failed to live up to their previous commitments. Therefore each manager tried to make his factory self-sufficient and as independent as possible of others for their supplies. Subcontracting was held to a minimum. This helped to make the manager immune to the failings of the Soviet transport system and the shortcomings of other manufacturers, but, as the proponents of economic reform noted, it resulted in the duplication of facilities and a form of domestic autarchy which denied the USSR many of the economic advantages which come with the division of labor.

Because waiting until the last minute is a universal trait, the *val* system also resulted in a very unbalanced production cycle. Like a student with a term-paper, no one cared at what specific time during the assignment period the task was completed as long as everything was finished at the zero hour on the last day. Consequently, in the Soviet factory, as in the dormitory, there seldom is much activity during the first twenty days of the month. In part, it is necessary to rest up from the rush of the last days of the preceding deadline. As a general rule, Russian factories consistently completed 50 to 70 per cent of their target during the last ten days of the month. This practice was called *storming*. Inevitably such behavior has undesirable effects: quality control of the goods being produced simply cannot be as rigid; shipping facilities are always jammed up once a month; and there is always the need for rest after the racing climax, which only causes a lag in meeting the following month's quota. This in turn is likely to mean another period of storming.

Fortunately for the manager, but not so fortunately for the state, no one seemed to care too much about quality control. In the first place, there seemed to be no suitable way to assign qualitative targets. Quality is often an intangible phenomenon. Moreover, when the state assigned a certain level of quality, the manager had no need and no desire to improve the quality of what he was making. Secondly, the pervading emphasis in all economic activity was on quantity. There seemed to be no other alternative if the Russians were to have the rapid economic growth they so desperately wanted. Such a result was inevitable when, for example, the national goals were broken down for each industrial factory. To fulfill his particular plan in as quick and easy a way as possible, the manager invariably looked for some shortcut that would allow him to complete his tasks on time. As we saw, this sometimes meant extravagance. On occasion, it might mean the opposite if the manager discovered that he could fulfill his output target and at the same time cut down his input costs. Thus, a cement plant manager might discover he could meet his tonnage target by increasing the cement's water content, the textile plant manager might find he could fulfill his yardage target by producing long thin strips of cloth, and the nail manufacturer might realize he could roll off his thousands of nails by making you know what.[4] Furthermore, if one abuse was corrected by a change in targets, the plant manager almost always seemed able to find some other shortcut. If the state wanted heavier nails and changed the target from number to tonnage, then the manufacturer would produce long fat nails.

Because the Soviet manager strained himself to fulfill and overfulfill his targets, this meant that he tried to avoid plant shutdowns or adjustments in production runs. Fortunately, the manager did not have to worry about whether anyone would buy his product. That was not his concern. The State Planning Commission (Gosplan), the organization ultimately responsible for assigning targets, had ordered the increase and presumably this meant that the order reflected a need for it elsewhere.[5] This was true for many years, but, as we shall see, by the early 1960s, this was not necessarily the case. It often turned out that increases in the production quotas were assigned out of habit rather than need. But that was Gosplan's problem. All the plant manager cared about was finding a steady source of supplies and turning out products. *Down time* to reset equipment for model changes was avoided wherever possible. Assigned quotas could not be filled if the production line was shut down in order to make adjustments in the product so it would better fit customer's needs. As a result, Soviet products often had a monotonous uniformity about them. Thus, Soviet men found it hard to buy anything but one style and, occasionally, only one size of blue underwear.

The planning authorities in Moscow were undisturbed by such practices and, in fact, stressed technological developments which moved in that direction. This proved to be a convenient arrangement since innovations of this type were easy to direct and guide from Moscow. For example, steel technology was much the same all over the country. There was not much need for local initiative by the manager on the scene. Gosplan and the Ministry of Steel could con-

[4] Small lightweight nails.
[5] Herbert S. Levine, "The Centralized Planning of Supply in Soviet Industry," *Comparisons of the United States and Soviet Economies,* prepared for the Joint Economic Committee, 86th Congress, 1st session, Washington, D.C.: U.S. Government Printing Office, 1959.

sequently sponsor research in enlarging blast furnace and open-hearth capacity and then put their findings to use throughout the country. It was something that everyone could benefit from, including the plant manager. Technological improvements of this sort made it possible for the manager to increase his production run of steel and, in the process, meet his output target with greater ease. This helps to explain why it was that the Russians were able to surpass the productive output of comparable blast furnaces and open-hearth furnaces in the United States. But it also meant that the customers of the steel mill found it hard to obtain more than one basic size and shape of steel. There was little or no concern about varying output to suit the customer if it meant disruption of the production process itself.

In the long run, the Soviet system discouraged innovation. Unless he had been assigned a priority project, few if any managers indicated any willingness to experiment with new products. Unless an innovation were to lead to increased production, nobody wanted to bother with it for fear that the production schedule would be disrupted and the plan underfulfilled. There was therefore little product or quality innovation at the plant level itself. There has even been occasional resistance to process innovation. Thus, the Russians have been even slower than their counterparts in the United States to introduce the highly efficient oxygen system of making steel.

The absence of new and better products in the production stream did not mean that there was no research being conducted. Quite the contrary; there was significant activity in the laboratories located throughout the country. As we have seen, the Russians were graduating well-trained scientists and engineers, and these technicians were busy inventing in their research institutes and laboratories. Still, even when something that was obviously quite attractive appeared, there was no way to ensure that the product would ever see the light of an assembly line or a retail shop. Unless it was a priority matter, most factory managers shunned the experimental products and techniques developed in the laboratory. But it was not just the factory manager who tried to avoid any undue risk, it was also the planners. They, too, found it much easier to point to a record of increased output for the units within their jurisdiction. Their record might be jeopardized if there was any experimentation with new products or processes.

It became gradually clear that centralized planning and the old

Soviet system of setting quantitative targets was not meant to cope with the sophisticated needs of certain sectors of the economy such as chemicals, electronics, computers, and consumer goods. When told to increase the country's production, the planners and managers simply added another blast furnace and increased the output of steel. If it happened that not steel, but specialized plastic and electronic products were needed, no one paid much attention. The planners still concentrated on steel because it was easier for central planners to plan increases in steel. As Khrushchev himself put it so colorfully,

> The production of steel is like a well-travelled road with deep ruts; here even blind horses will not turn off because the wheels will break. Similarly some officials have put on steel blinkers; they do everything as they were taught in their day. A material appears which is superior to steel and is cheaper, but they keep on shouting "Steel, steel." [6]

Khrushchev was asking if it really was such a good thing to have the world's highest output per blast furnace but virtually no plastic, computer, or fertilizer industries.

Given such a conservative atmosphere, it was very difficult to introduce radical change. The innovations that had been generated were almost always the result of a massive campaign. This was apparently the only way that the Soviet government could jolt its planners and managers. The best illustration of this was in 1963 when Khrushchev suddenly realized that, if he wanted better things for better living, he would have to find them through chemistry. But how do you build a chemical industry overnight? Khrushchev used all the power and propaganda of the state. He even tampered with some original and sacred gospels. Lenin's injunction that "Communism is the Soviet system plus the electrification of the entire country" was altered to read, "Communism is the Soviet system plus the electrification of the entire country, plus the chemicalization of agriculture." Capital expenditures of $45 billion over a four-year period were promised. Nothing was considered new or modern unless it involved some association with chemistry. In 1964, it was a shock to find even Moscow's

[6] *Pravda,* Nov. 20, 1962, p. 4.

taxi drivers reading chemistry textbooks in their spare time. The campaign method had its obvious shortcomings, but the old incentive system made it virtually impossible to induce innovation and change in any other way.

It was with much the same abandon that the Russians undertook some of their impressive construction projects, though their enthusiasm often exceeded the bounds of economic rationality. Because Soviet planners were not constrained by the restrictions of an interest rate calculation, they were able to proceed on the assumption that capital was a free good. When anything is free, it is used in large quantities. Even though the state had monopolized the task of capital formation and seemed to be doing very well in its efforts, capital was still in very short supply in the Soviet Union relative to the possible uses to which it could be put. Because of their prestige and political power the dam and subway builders had virtually no economic limit on what they could ask for. They were able to obtain almost all the capital they wanted. This in turn meant that the shortages of capital were even greater in other areas with less political but possibly more economic importance.

Lack of economic restraint in capital project-building can often be very dangerous. Khrushchev himself acknowledged this when he deplored the fact that so much priority had been given to hydroelectric projects. Eventually he realized that the construction of less spectacular but cheaper thermal or coal-generated electricity would have made more economic sense. Similarly, many others have confessed that the cost of the whole Volga–Don canal network has not been warranted by the economic use to which it has been put. In reflecting on this penchant for massive water construction projects, Peter Wiles has observed that there is almost something Freudian about water and economic planners embarked on a crash program of economic development.[7] To the planner, the measure of economic progress is the size of the dams and canals he builds. (Reportedly, Stalin also favored canals because he felt, in this way, his work could be appreciated on Mars.) Consequently, enormous monuments are erected which generally bear no economic fruit for many years to come. If any meaningful economic value were attached to capital, many of those projects

[7] Peter Wiles, *The Political Economy of Communism.* Cambridge, Mass.: Harvard University Press, 1962, p. 99.

96

would have either been postponed or designed on a much smaller scale.

Although the campaign method may be fun for someone who likes excitement, it is not a very satisfactory way to run an economy. Inevitably, there is only so much that the planners and ministers in Moscow can concentrate on and promote. This means that there are gaps and discontinuities in the productive process and in the mix of goods made available. It is this more than anything else that explains why trivial products such as ball-point pens, pencil sharpeners and scotch tape, not to mention those basic necessities of life, the electric can opener and the T.V. dinner were generally unavailable in the Soviet Union as late as 1967. No one at the all-republic level had ever decided they were worth producing. Since a manager at a local factory could not or would not risk the production of such things, such goods simply did not exist. Analyzing the problem, one Soviet economist argued that the situation would not improve until "Moscow stops telling the cooks in Vladivostok how to make borsch."

Because the Russians fell so far behind Western technology in the nonpriority areas, they began to rely on imports to close the gap. In many ways this must have been a humiliating experience because exactly the same tactic had been relied upon in the 1920s and 1930s. Presumably, in the interim, the Russians should have been able to move rapidly ahead so that Russian technology would be equal to or more advanced than that in Western Europe or Japan. But it did not work out that way. Instead, Kosygin has now declared that it was inefficient to pirate foreign products. In his opinion, the effort expended in trying to find the production secrets and technical know-how of various foreign products was more costly in money and time than buying the factory and know-how outright. Kosygin estimated that the purchase of patent rights abroad will save the USSR hundreds of millions of dollars in scientific research during the Five-Year Plan of 1966 to 1970.[8]

If the physical planning system has all the inefficiencies that have been suggested, why was it used in the first place? Would it not have been wiser to rely on the traditional forms of motivation, i.e., the price and profit systems? Traditionally, private owners of factories in

[8] *Pravda,* Apr. 6, 1966, p. 7.

Western industrialized countries had not concerned themselves particularly about their country's economic growth. A manager could normally accomplish his own ends best by selling more of his product and increasing his production. As an incidental by-product, this increased the country's gross national product. Western managers' efforts to ensure profit for themselves had brought about a fairly balanced, well-adjusted growth, and the system seemed to be self-correcting. Changes in taste and demand were rapidly transmitted by a "feedback" system to the factory manager who acted quickly to maximize his profit; overexpansion was immediately indicated by a fall in sales, a change in prices, formation of excess inventory, and a fall in profit.

This rather precise but uncoordinated control through prices and profits did not appeal to Soviet planners. As we have seen, they were more concerned about massive change than careful adjustment. They wanted to open the throttle wide. The slow and not always sure methods of industrialization that had been used in the West would simply not do. This led them to adopt the severe and draconic forms of central planning we have just discussed. This also meant that they had to ignore many of the signals of the traditional profit system. Failure to insulate the economy from such signals would have made it impossible to build up the country's heavy industry. The population would have preferred light industry and consumer goods and they would have been willing to pay high prices for such goods. In turn, this would have meant high profits. To ensure that this did not happen, prices had to be controlled strictly. This also explains why the profits of an enterprise were made subordinate to output targets.

Once the state engages in manipulation of this sort, all kinds of imbalances result. The temptation of high but illegal profits gives rise to antisocial activities in the form of private production and sale as well as stealing from the state. The more state planners and managers disregard these illegal high prices and profits, the more removed from reality the official economic guideposts become and the more difficult it is to reduce the degree of central planning. Thus, the desire for consumer goods in the Soviet Union was frustrated by underpricing products of heavy industry and overpricing goods for the consumer. A turnover or sales tax was imposed on consumer goods which, on the average, doubled their price. No such tax was imposed on heavy industrial products. If anything, subsidies were provided to encourage the use of such products. Similarly, no long-term interest rate was charged, and most enterprises and farms paid no significant rent. Occasionally hidden rent and interest would be charged through the device of differentiated prices or turnover taxes, but, generally, these efforts were not fully effective. Consequently, central controls of some sort had to be maintained until something was done to restructure the makeup of production so that consumer tastes could be better satisfied. Only then could profits and prices serve as meaningful guides to the actions sought by the state. Of course, without using prices and profits as a determinant for production, it is hard to determine just how distorted the economic balance might be. But allowing prices and profits to serve as actual guides means that there might be chaos, at least initially. It is a hard circle to break.[9]

Agriculture

Industry is not the only area of economic inefficiency in the Soviet economy. Whatever can be said about Soviet industrial problems can be repeated about the Soviet agricultural problems. But whereas the Russians have had impressive industrial successes to offset their industrial shortcomings, there is virtually nothing to boast about in agriculture. At the same time that the fifty-year Communist Party statement shows the multifold expansion in the output of such commodities as steel, oil, electricity, and refrigerators, it must be with some embarrassment that it can show an increase of only 1.8 times in the harvest of grain since 1940, an increase of 2.3 times in the production of meat, and an increase of 3.1 times in the production of butter.[10] There did seem to be some progress from 1953 to 1958. Similarly 1966 and 1967 seemed to be good crop years. But on the whole, the successes have not balanced the failures. As an indication of just how far productivity in Soviet agriculture lags behind that of

[9] Morris Bornstein, "The Soviet Price System," *American Economic Review*, Mar. 1962, p. 64; also, Gregory Grossman, "Industrial Prices in the USSR," *American Economic Review*, May, 1959, p. 50.
[10] *Pravda*, June 25, 1967.

the United States, it is interesting to note that in the United States, about 6 farmers provide more than enough food for 100 people. In the USSR, however, it takes about 40 farmers to supply 100 people. In other words, the Russians need more than six times the number of farmers required in the United States and even then there often is not enough food to go around.

Many factors can be found to explain Russia's problem in agriculture. It is tempting and fairly accurate to blame the present Soviet difficulties on the decision to collectivize the land. If nothing else, this led to the destructive slaughter of livestock and other capital stock that has not been completely remedied even today. Conceivably, if the Russians had embarked on a massive program of capital investment in agriculture right after collectivization, their agricultural problems would not have been so widespread nor so prolonged in their effect. But no such investment was made. In Khrushchev's time, more attention was devoted to agriculture, but Khrushchev always seemed to have been entranced by some "get rich quick" scheme that never seemed to work out. First, he spent millions of rubles on developing the virgin lands in Kazakhstan. This area had been little used before, however, for good reasons; it lacked adequate rainfall and a long enough growing season. The virgin lands did provide some badly needed grain, especially in the mid-1950s. But ultimately Khrushchev got what he should have realized he would get, a little dustbowl. Moreover the economist must always ask what was the economic cost of such a project? The enormous costs that were required to erect new cities and farms was hardly worth the uncertain return.

Trying to make up for Stalin's neglect, Khrushchev kept adopting new schemes. Taking a hint from America's experience, he thought for a time that corn would be Russia's salvation. He ordered that virtually every farm grow some corn. Again, the climatic conditions did not suit the needs of corn, and the project was similarly abandoned. In the aftermath of this experience, there emerged some pathetic tales of misdirected zeal. For example, some officials insisted that corn even be planted in the Ural Mountains and the far north, where it is a struggle even to grow wheat. Khrushchev next decided that it was a waste of resources to allow farm land to lie fallow.

Assuming that fertilizer would be available to nourish the land, he ordered all fallow and meadowland put into cultivation. The fertilizer was unavailable, and the productivity of the land suffered. Khrushchev's successors have not been entirely convinced of the folly of projects like this. In 1966 they launched their own campaign of amelioration or drying-out of meadow and swamp land and the irrigation of dry land. These were all measures that increased production, but, as always, at a very high cost.

American farm experts feel that a more productive policy would be to follow some of the other measures that have produced such a high return in the United States. They argue that the Russians should direct their investment into the production of hybrid seed. This highly productive seed should then be used in conjunction with increased qualities of fertilizer. To bring the enlarged crops to market, foreign agronomists also insist that the Russians should then construct an extensive road network of farm-to-market highways. As it is now, it is impossible for the farmer to move freely and rapidly across the vast distances of the Soviet Union. The dirt roads turn into mud beds at the first thaw or rainfall. All of these measures involve tremendous costs. Before fertilizer can be produced, a chemical industry must be created. Similarly, before the farmer will be able to use the roads, there must be a massive expansion of the truck industry and the construction industry. In 1965, there were about 700,000 miles of roadway, of which only about 200,000 miles had a hard surface.[11] In contrast there were over 3,600,000 miles of highway in the United States in 1964, of which only 900,000 were classified as unsurfaced.[12] The Russians obviously have a long way to go if they ever hope to provide the same kind of mobility that is available to the American farmer.

Concerning highway construction, the Russians are somewhat more fortunate than the Americans in that there is no need to construct highways over much of the area because the land is unsuited for agriculture. Despite the immensity of the Soviet land mass, only a portion of the land is either not too cold or not too hot or not too

[11] *Nar. Khoz, 1965,* p. 493.
[12] U.S. Bureau of the Census, *Statistical Abstract of the United States: 1966,* 87th ed., Washington, D.C., 1966, p. 562.

dry or not too wet. But while this makes it easier for the highway construction officials, it does not ease the task of the Ministry of Agriculture.

Yet, no matter how important is the contribution of capital investment in agriculture and the improvement of seeds, fertilizer and highways, the big obstacle is still the lack of enthusiasm and even resistance of the peasants. The peasants feel they have been taken advantage of and are reluctant to do their best. Recognizing the passive resistance of the peasants, the Soviet government under Brezhnev and Kosygin has recently been increasing incentive payments just as Khrushchev did in the mid-1950s. As a result farm incomes have risen more rapidly than urban incomes in the mid-1960s. Just as the rapid rise of farmers' income in the mid-1950s had a positive effect on increasing production, so there was a similar impact a decade later. Among the actions taken was the decision to lift some of the restrictions regulating the use of the peasant's private plot. Realizing that produce from the private plot is an important means of improving consumption for the urban sector, the state is actually encouraging peasants to bring more to market. After all, although they made up only 3 per cent of all the cultivated land area, in 1964 the private plots accounted for 42 per cent of the country's milk and meat production, 73 per cent of the egg output, and 60 per cent of the potato harvest.[13]

Similarly, the promise of pensions for the collective farmer has done much to raise morale. The knowledge that he will be cared for in his old age makes the peasant more willing to work in his younger years. But the most important measure, except for the increase in the procurement price of food products, has been the decision to make the collective farmer less of a risk bearer. This was done to increase the peasant's trust in the regime. In the future the peasant is to receive a significant portion of his salary in advance of the harvest. This will make him more like a regular wage earner, that is, like the farmers on the *sovkhoz,* the state farms. In fact, some authorities sense that the collective farms are gradually being turned into state farms. This in itself will probably not solve the farm problem, but it should make the average collective farmer's life more secure.

Ironically, some authorities in the West are beginning to acknowl-

[13] *Nar. Khoz., 1965,* p. 288; *Soviet News,* Mar. 25, 1966, p. 152.

102

edge that the *sovkhoz* (state farms) might some day be able to solve Russia's farm problem. For many years, most foreign authorities agreed that the only successful farm was the family farm as it exists in the United States. Only in a setting like the family farm, it was argued, would it be possible to stimulate the farmer to work the long, hard hours necessary to care for the varied needs that exist in agriculture. Moreover, since farming was more or less like a closed cycle of production, the farm had to be diversified. Only in this way could the farmer's time and the by-products of farming such as manure and hay be used as efficiently as possible. All of this would only be possible if the farmer were motivated by the lure of private profits. With the family farm as a model, it was pretty clear that neither the *kolkhoz* (the collective farm) nor the *sovkhoz* (the state farm) would ever be efficient.

The change in expert opinion about the *sovkhoz* is not due to any sudden increase in efficiency; rather, the American family farm no longer looks as idyllic or as advantageous as it once did. With the advent of hybrid seed, fertilizer, and large-scale automation, American agriculture even more than Soviet agriculture has undergone a revolution. Today diversified farming is no longer so important in American agriculture. There are farms which produce nothing but hogs or chicken or cattle or corn. Moreover, because of the introduction of so much mechanized equipment, the work is now often performed during regularly scheduled hours by hired help who work for pay on an hourly basis like factory workers in the city. If and when similar techniques and capital are introduced into Soviet agriculture, the Russians should be able to obtain the same results. However, given the existing lack of capital on the Soviet farm and the bitterness that the Soviet farmer still feels for the state, this may be some time in coming.

Other Resources

The Russians have not been too much more successful in their use of other natural resources. As in agriculture, the Russians have often placed too little emphasis on the proper use of their resources and therefore they have been used poorly. To some extent, this comes as a surprise, because, as we mentioned earlier, the Russians claim that their system has done away with the wasteful duplication of private competition. Theoretically, therefore, everything in the USSR should be judged on whether it leads to the most efficient use of the state's resources.

Soviet theory notwithstanding, the fact is that economic activity in the USSR is carried out by state-owned enterprises. Since they are striving mightily to fulfill their planned targets, they often act as any firm in the United States might act. The Soviet manager is primarily interested in fulfilling his target, and he tends to disregard anything else which has no impact on his success. Thus, if the state planner is able to provide for the proper use of natural resources in the manager's target, the manager will use the natural resources with care. If no such provision is made, then he will take for granted whatever resources are involved and, if need be, neglect or destroy them. Soviet oil drilling firms engage in slant-drilling oil for the purpose of drawing on oil pools that belong to other firms.[14] This is inefficient and lowers the ultimate output of the oil basin. Supposedly such waste occurs only in the free enterprise system.

Similarly, the proper use of air and water is not normally considered an important variable in the production target of the enterprise. If it is cheaper to return the air and water in dirtier form than it was originally, the enterprise manager will consequently not bother to clean it. The manager would have to expend time and money to clean such resources. This would interfere with his attempt to fulfill the plan or make a profit. For this reason, air and water pollution are also major problems in the USSR.

Some of the instances of pollution in the Soviet Union are actually as serious as anything that has happened recently in the United States. Lake Baikal in Siberia is the deepest lake in the world, deeper even than Lake Tahoe. For that reason, it is a treasure trove of sea life. Moreover, because the land surrounding it has been uninhabited for so long, the lake has not been affected by human pollution. Also, because the area has been uninhabited, it has rich and untouched timber stands. Someone in Moscow ultimately realized that these acres

[14] For further examples, see *Trud,* Aug. 12, 1967, p. 2.

of virgin timber and gallons of fresh water would make an excellent site for a paper mill. So a town was built and a paper mill erected. It happens, however, that paper mills are one of the worst polluters in the world. If nothing else, just cutting the timber along the lakeshore to build the factory and the town has precipitated erosion and silt formation that have caused trouble regardless of how pure the effluent of the paper factory may turn out to be. Despite emotional pleas of Russian and foreign conservationists, the city and plant were built, and the unclean discharge is now being emptied into the lake. Thus, like Lake Tahoe, Lake Baikal is being polluted; but, unlike Lake Tahoe, Lake Baikal is being polluted by a state institution with the state's approval.

There are numerous other instances of pollution in the USSR. One-third of all the rivers in the Ukraine are polluted. The problem is not much better elsewhere in the country. Over 60 per cent of the cities and towns and 65 per cent of the industrial firms in the Russian Republic lack purifying facilities, and, therefore, they do not treat their sewage. It should not come as a surprise, consequently, that large cities like Vladimir, Voronezh, Orenburg, and Tiumen lack adequate supplies of drinking water.[15]

In much the same way, conservationists began to complain in mid-1966 that one of the country's most famous resort areas was being despoiled. For many years, Kislovodsk had been regarded as one of nature's wonders. Located in the Caucasus mountains, it was protected on three sides from the cold north winds. The only open side was on a long valley to the south through which flowed a constant supply of clean, warm air. Normally Kislovodsk recorded 311 days of sun a year. Just over the northern side of the mountains, Piatigorsk had only 122 days of sun. The rest were either full of wind, fog, rain, or snow.

Unfortunately, after World War II, someone in the railroad ministry built a limestone converter at Podkumok just over the mountains to the north of Kislovodsk. Because the planners and manager of the limestone converter sought to make an ever more favorable impression, production at the plant was increased, and, by 1966, eight furnaces were in operation. In the constant effort to meet the

[15] *Ekonomicheskaia Gazeta,* **4,** January, 1967, p. 37.

government plan, more and more limestone was smelted until a channel had been dug through the mountains. In the quest for a valuable raw material, a priceless international heritage was being destroyed. Already in 1966 the dust in the air at Kislovodsk exceeded by 1.5 times the norm prescribed for a nonresort city.

Anyone who is familiar with the problems of pollution in the United States knows that somewhat similar examples of destruction and lack of foresight can be found in this country. But the Russians have two special considerations they must contend with that actually make their problems harder to solve. First of all, the state in the USSR acts much less as a middleman between the polluter and the public. As in our discussion of what happens when the state is the owner of all industry, we find that, in fact, the state is often the villain itself, the polluter. This applies not only to municipal waste, but to industrial waste. The success and reputation of the local government and party officials are primarily dependent on the economic production record of their area. Like the factory manager, the more production is increased, the better it is for their records. As yet no official index of pollution prevention has been designed for incorporation into the manager's calculations. Since the manager and the local government officials are primarily interested in expanding production, anything that interferes with that growth is considered a disruption and a threat. Consequently, local government and Party officials are generally unsympathetic to pleas from conservationists and other concerned citizens. In effect, therefore, the government is much less of a middleman between the polluter and the affected, and more of a polluter itself than it is in this country.

There is a second consideration. Until recently, the Russians have not made an explicit calculation for rent. Inevitably this has contributed to the improper utilization of land. Just as we saw that the Russian manager acted as if capital were free and unlimited when no charge was made for the use of capital, so Russian managers have acted as if the land and natural resources were free. Minerals have been mined and priced without proper recognition of the advantages of location and richness of the ore. This has resulted in excessive demands being placed on some materials and lack of exploitation of others. As an example, wherever possible, enterprises in the western part of the USSR tried to obtain raw materials from nearby mines.

106

Because transportation costs on these products were cheaper and the minerals themselves normally included no markup for rent, the price of using such materials was relatively cheaper than bringing in minerals from Siberia. For the same reasons, consumers of Soviet raw materials in Eastern Europe also preferred to use raw materials from western Russia. Eventually Russian officials began to realize their resources in the western part of the USSR were being depleted. They also realized that, in satisfying the orders of the Eastern Europeans, the Russians themselves were having to develop new and expensive mines in Siberia. Moreover, they complained, shorter distance and therefore lower transportation costs for the raw materials in the west meant that no one wanted to use the raw materials from Siberia. Therefore several Russian economists began to call for higher charges (rent) for the materials which were located closer to the market.[16]

Land Usage

A similar policy has led to improper planting of agricultural products. Until recently little recognition was taken of the proximity of a farm to the city. Consequently, because of the absence of rent and a poor pricing policy, there was no mechanism except a direct administrative dictate to ensure that vegetables, fruits, and milk would be produced near cities and wheat crops in more distant locations.

Although there are many more variables, somewhat the same forces help to explain some of the city-planning problems that exist in the USSR. Here again, however, there is no guarantee that the use of rent will ensure the end of poor city planning. City planning continues to be a problem in countries where rent is charged. In fact, sometimes the complaint is made that the quest for high rents leads to poor city planning. But, while efforts to maximize rent collections may lead to improper land usage, lack of rent may lead to the same result. As it is, every Soviet ministry wants to locate not only its offices in and around Moscow, but also its factories. Higher rents and land values would lead to the location of these factories in out-

[16] *Voprosy Ekonomiki,* Apr. 1966, p. 89; also, *Voprosy Ekonomiki,* May, 1966, p. 87.

lying areas where it is less congested. In the same way, stores are often located at ill-chosen sites. With great fanfare the Russians opened the new and modern Moskva Department Store in the new and fancy Southwest region of the city. For some strange reason, the store was not located at a transportation junction. It was surrounded by many high-rise apartments, but it should have been realized that this would not provide enough of a buying clientele. Because of the absence of customer traffic, the store simply lacked the potential patronage of stores like GUM and TsUM in downtown Moscow. Consequently, for some time, the Moskva had difficulty earning a profit. More realistic resource allocation policy would have helped guide Soviet trade officials to a better location.

REALITY: *Like any industrialized economy, the Soviet economy is a delicate instrument that requires fine tuning at numerous points. Inevitably there is bound to be some disharmony since even the best instruments sometimes lose their pitch. In the USSR, the overcentralized system of administration that was in effect until 1965 led to more distortion than perhaps would have taken place under an alternative economic system. As the economy grew in size, it simply became impossible to centralize all decision making in Moscow. Among the main problems were a lack of innovation and unwise use of natural resources.*

PART IV

The Role
of Ideology
in Day-to-Day
Economic
Operations

MYTH: *Marxism is a vital force in the day to day conduct of economic activity in the Soviet Union. All the old capitalistic forms have been tossed into the trash basket of history.*

Whatever the dreams of the revolutionaries or others who have felt oppressed by the economic structures which enveloped them, they soon discovered that it is one thing to dream and another thing to assume responsibility. In the words of the cynic, "It is easy to philosophize, but what philosopher has ever met a payroll?"

As soon as he took control after the Revolution, Lenin realized he had to meet the payroll. Instead of calling for destruction, he suddenly began to advocate construction. Moreover, the society he was trying to construct was a heavily industrialized one. As we have seen, an industrialized economy has its own imperatives, which can only be met in a limited number of ways. Like it or not, if too many of the traditional institutional arrangements for running the mechanism are discarded, there will be extravagance and inefficiency.

At this point it might be worthwhile to pause a bit over the concept of capitalism. As others have pointed out in the past, the word when used to differentiate the American economy from the Soviet economy is a misnomer. Technically, capitalism refers to any state that uses large quantities of capital in its production process. This is opposed to a primitive agrarian society or a handicraft culture. In other words, any country which is industrialized, by definition uses large quantities of capital and theoretically is a capitalist country.

Strictly speaking, if the farmer uses large quantities of capital, even agricultural societies like New Zealand and Denmark could be considered capitalistic.

Because the Soviet Union is an industrialized society where capital investments are regarded as priority matters, it could be said that the Soviet Union is capitalist just as is Japan, the United Kingdom, or the United States. Note that nothing has been said about who owns the capital. That is a different issue and clearly there is a distinction here. When the word capitalism itself is used, it could refer either to state capitalism (the USSR) or private capitalism (the USA).

The pause for this semantic distinction was made for a specific purpose. Because it is an industrialized or capitalized society, the USSR has to contend with numerous problems that closely resemble problems found in any capitalized state. In the same way, the mother-child relationship is remarkably similar whatever the social forms and, for that matter, for most of the species. Thus the Russian economic planners like their counterparts elsewhere have to worry about all the old economic questions: What should be produced, how much of it, and for whom? This involves determinations such as which plant should be sent what raw materials when, which worker should be trained for what specialty, what new process technique and product should replace existing techniques and products, and how much should be set aside from existing consumption for future growth. No matter what one's ideology, these questions must be answered. The range of possible questions is endless, and the variation in answers is just as long. If the wrong questions and the wrong answers are to be avoided, experience has shown that certain guides can be of considerable help. Failure to use all of these guides need not lead to catastrophe. Nonetheless, as the economic structure becomes more and more complex and its parts become more interrelated, even the Russians have found that their rejection of these guides has been at considerable cost.

After the initial euphoria of the revolution, Lenin and Stalin sat down to the *business* of making their economy grow. Some economic devices they decided could be eliminated. Largely for ideological reasons, they denied the existence of an interest rate and rent. They also reduced the significance of profit as a motivating and guiding factor.

We have seen how the Russians managed to do quite well for a

112

time without interest, rent, and profit. They were able to disregard the normal signals provided by such economic indicators and take what they considered to be the massive strides necessary to accelerate their march toward forced industrialization. Implicit in their action was the realization that there was so much to be done that the application of capital would most likely provide an increase in production no matter where it was applied. Although they might not have selected those investments with for example a 30 per cent return on capital, they could still be content if their administrative methods led them to select projects with a lower return, say only 20 per cent. In either case, there would be rapid growth. Their main goal was capital accumulation and the question of internal and external economies of scale. They were not interested in precision since they concluded there was more to be gained by broad sweeping measures than precise but hesitant and timid steps. Even those projects where the returns were negative could be offset by the economies of scale elsewhere. Somewhat later, as the industrialized sector began to grow and there were fewer investment opportunities with high rates of return, such hit-or-miss methods ceased to be adequate. Then it became a question of a 15 per cent versus a 12 per cent rate of return, and it was important that the most productive project be selected. It was realized that a return to some of the prerevolutionary techniques would be necessary even though this meant a loss of ideological purity.

The experience with prices was somewhat the same. Presumably, in a state of communism, there would be no price system. In fact, the Russians soon realized that they could not dispense with prices. The decision was nonetheless made to circumscribe their effect and make prices as well as profits suit the requirements of direct planning. The most important commodities in the economy were routed according to the orders of Gosplan. Prices like profits were treated as a secondary consideration. If the price of a product was too high, it would be reduced and a subsidy supplied to finance the difference. At the same time, because of excess purchasing power, the turnover tax was applied to jack up the prices of consumer goods. But since even a 100 per cent tax was generally inadequate to breech the gap between supply and demand, the final solution to the problem was to leave the shelves empty and force the consumers to form queues for that which was available. Indicative of how little importance the planners attached to prices was the practice of allowing only infrequent price changes. There were periods of five or ten years during which no major change in industrial prices was permitted. Prices did have importance on the fringes of society such as at the collective farm markets. Also prices of some surplus industrial goods were allowed to fluctuate, but generally prices were regarded as a subsidiary tool, at best.

In the same fashion, the Communists attempted to nullify the effect of some other economic devices. Invariably, they had considerably less success. For a time Stalin supported the idea that there should be equalization of wages. It did not take him long to see, however, that, regardless of what Marxist theory had to say about how the proletariat were supposed to act, in fact they wanted differentiated wages. If a man worked harder or performed a more complex and skilled task, he expected to be paid more for his effort. It soon became apparent that, without incentives and therefore differentiated pay, there were few who would accept extra responsibility or training. Consequently, the policy of wage leveling was replaced by a policy of wage differentiation. Moreover, the Soviet tax system tends to accentuate this policy of differentiation. As we saw, the main form of taxation is the turnover or sales tax, which of necessity falls especially hard on lower income groups. At the same time, the upper income groups escape with considerably more of their income intact. This is due to the absence of a Soviet inheritance tax and to the effect of a progressive income tax that never rises above 13 per cent for state-employed workers and managers. (The high sales tax, low income tax, and no inheritance tax are remarkably close to the tax program advocated by the John Birch Society.) Periodically, there have been efforts to eliminate some of the extremes in income, but no attempt has been made to fulfill the ideological dream that all men would earn equal incomes or, as Marx put it, "From each according to his ability, to each according to his needs."

In contrast to the efforts made to diminish the importance of interest, rent, prices, profit, and wage differentials, Stalin never found it necessary or possible to abolish some of the other economic mechanisms. From an ideological point of view, the most anomalous set of institutions which has prevailed throughout the whole 50-year pe-

114

riod is the banking system and money and credit. After all, money and banking as much as anything have stood for the main symbols of private capitalism. Yet, from the beginning, few if any responsible Soviet leaders seriously thought that the Soviet Union could eliminate banks or money. Why?

Let us take money first. The alternative to money is barter. Anyone who has tried to carry on anything more complicated than the exchange of baseball cards knows how difficult it would be to conduct one's daily affairs without money. Ration coupons could be used, but that, after all, is just a more restricted form of money. Admittedly, money may not be important in the conduct of activity between industrial enterprises. We saw how goods can be allocated, at least up to a certain point, on the basis of a physical plan drawn up by Gosplan; but it would be impossible for Gosplan to prescribe the precise consumption activities of every citizen. Consequently, it is easier and cheaper to decentralize the whole operation and allow the individual to spend and purchase as he pleases from among the goods that have been made available for him. Conceivably, some day there will be such abundance that everyone will be able to take what he wants without any need to worry about rationing. However, modern day experience indicates that today's luxuries have a way of becoming tomorrow's necessities. It is consequently hard to see how there will ever be such abundance that goods will be available for the asking. Accordingly, money will continue to serve as a device for allocating the limited supply of goods to a population with limitless demands.

What about Gosbank, the Soviet banking network? It should be fairly evident that, with all that money, you need a bank in which to put it. Actually it is not so much the cash that is circulating among individuals that creates the need for banks, as it is the clearing and checking accounts that circulate among enterprises. Just as in the United States, checking deposits in the USSR constitute more than 80 per cent of all the money supply. Consequently, some kind of institution, be it a bank or a clearing house, is needed to handle the paper work. But Gosbank has gone beyond the mere bookkeeping function of balancing accounts. It is also a supplier of short-term credit. How can this be explained? Why is it that a state-owned firm

115

in the USSR needs credit? It needs it for the same reason that a business anyplace in the world needs credit—because production takes place in advance of the sale. As a result, funds must be made available to pay for salaries and supplies until the anticipated revenues from the sale of the product can be collected. Conceivably, each enterprise could be provided with an initial endowment of working capital to tide it over its peak periods. However, this would necessitate needlessly large sums of capital that would either be left idle for the remainder of the year or create a temptation for some unauthorized use. In any case, it would be a waste of resources.

Similar analysis helps to explain the vitality of such Soviet institutions as savings banks, insurance, and patents and copyrights. To reduce the threat of inflation and to provide a safe place for personal savings, the Russians have a wide network of savings banks. In 1966, there were approximately 74,000 such banks. Deposits totaled over $20 billion. Depending on the type of account the saver chooses, he can earn up to 3 per cent a year on his deposit. In the same way, accidents and destruction occur in every society. Consequently, individuals tend to seek some kind of protection for their property by pooling together a portion of their assets and insuring themselves so that, in case of an accident, provision will have been made for some of the cost. In this way, they seek to prevent the full burden from falling heavily on any one individual. To encourage the search for new ideas and concepts, the Soviet Union also provides patent and copyright recognition. Although the rewards are not as lucrative as in the Western world, the fact remains that they have found that even limited payment of rewards for patents and copyrights stimulates the exploration of new ideas. Finally, the Russians have provision for bankruptcy. After a little reflection, this should not seem so odd. Inevitably, there must be stores with bad managers or factories with obsolete products. Sometimes the store may have a good manager but what can he do when suddenly all his customers move away because the neighborhood is razed for urban renewal. Subsidies cannot be paid to such enterprises forever, especially if it happens that their product is not a necessary one.

For the socialist who is pure of mind, the preceding enumeration of capitalistic mechanisms at work in the USSR is probably a major disappointment. But disappointment is nothing in comparison to the shock that will come from finding out what has been going on in the USSR since September, 1965.

The Need for Reforms

As has been mentioned several times before, economic growth brings with it increasing complexity. The economic organism becomes not only larger in size but more complex. The number of possible interrelationships grows at a multiple rate. If this growth is accompanied by rapid technological change, the problems of administering this evolving colossus are immense.

Throughout most of the plan era, the underlying assumption in the USSR has been that everything would and could be planned from Moscow. We have shown how this was done with some success, at least for a limited period of time. But the centralized approach could carry the Russians only so far. The people in Intourist, the Russian travel organization, could have told the planners what to expect. For several years, the Russians insisted that every foreign tourist in the USSR be provided with a personal guide. There was a double purpose for such a policy: this way the tourist could be shown and be seen. But, as the number of tourists in the Soviet Union began to grow by the tens of thousands, it simply became impossible to give each one personal attention. Inevitably, there had to be some decentralization of control, and of necessity some tourists had to be left to their own devices. They could be provided with broad guidelines, but not individual guides.

The task of administrating an increasingly complex organism is not unique to the USSR or to Soviet industry. Institutions in the West and particularly the United States have also had to contend with this situation. Some large firms have found they cannot solve their problems and find that the economies of scale they gain from increasing productive or selling capacity are more than offset by diseconomies of scale in administration. American enterprises were lucky in that, just when they needed help after a period of rapid expansion, new techniques for extending managerial control were made available (or perhaps, because the new technology had been developed, the firms

117

were able to expand). Beginning in the 1950s, computers were made available for commercial use, and significant improvements were made in the field of communications. Initially, the computers were used primarily as data collecting and sorting devices. (Only later was there much use of the computer as a problem solver.) This made it possible to administer enlarged organizational units. Moreover, because of the speed and thoroughness of the computers, in many cases it became possible to supply information to management that was superior and more easily digested than before the expansion. For example, many enterprises today have better inventory control than they had before. Also, because of the increased use and flexibility of private wires or no-limit telephone service (WATS), this information can be transmitted more rapidly between the periphery and the center.

Unfortunately for the Russians, their economy was growing in size and complexity, but there was no companion increase in the use of data processing or improved communication. When such material becomes more widely available, then perhaps there can be a resumption of increased control at the center, that is, on the assumption that the economy does not jump off into a more complex form again. In the absence of better control equipment, the Russians have been forced to decentralize some of their efforts.

They have also had to revise some of their managerial stimuli. Increasingly, it became apparent that what was good for the manager and his enterprise was not necessarily good for the country as a whole. As we have seen, until 1965, Soviet managers were assigned physical plan targets. Fulfillment of those targets determined the size of the manager's bonus as well as the bonus of his employees. This resulted in ever-increasing production, which was just what the central planners considered to be their over-all national goal. They wanted production for production's sake. Gradually, however, the central planners began to realize that there had been a change in conditions and that somehow Soviet managers at almost all levels were no longer promoting the national good. Even though the manager at the plant level was doing his job as well as before and was responding to the traditional stimuli, the quality and variety of the goods being produced were not what they should have been. Unexpected inventories began to pile up and the rate of economic growth began to slow down. Yet most Soviet managers were not being deliberately disruptive. It was like trying to cool a hot room when the thermostat is placed near the window; the more the window is opened, the hotter the room becomes. The Soviet manager, like the thermostat, was doing as instructed, but what he was doing was wrong in the broader context of the nation's welfare. In fact, the better the manager performed according to the existing success criteria which had been designed for him at the plant level, the worse the national situation became and the higher the stock of useless products.

The remedy for such a malaise lay in revamping the whole incentive and planning system. This was due in large part to the efforts of Professor Evsei Liberman and his supporters, such as V. S. Nemchinov, L. V. Kantorovich, and V. A. Trapeznikov. Those who advocated reform saw important shortcomings in the existing economic system. Just as we have noted, they saw that capital was being used badly. Projects were not always selected rationally and, once chosen, they often required too much time to complete. Inevitably this adversely affected economic growth. For that matter, the whole emphasis on physical output targets created a host of distortions throughout the economy. For example, because they feared they would underfulfill their plan if the targets were set too high, the managers often concentrated on means to outsmart the planner rather than improve their production. For much the same reasons, we saw how the factory manager sought to make their factories as self-contained as possible. Managers also sought to build up buffer stocks of supplies for the same reason, i.e., in order to protect themselves from the shortcomings of others. There always seemed to be a tautness and general shortage of goods throughout the economy.[1] In fact, because of hoarding, supplies were needlessly short. Reflecting the idle reserves, Soviet inventory to sales ratios were actually higher than similar ratios in the United States.[2] Finally, the pressure to storm, that we described earlier, generated needless waste and confusion.

Whatever the criticisms of the existing system, no one would have paid any attention if economic growth had continued as before. How-

[1] Holland Hunter, "Optimum Tautness in Developmental Planning," *Economic Development and Cultural Change,* July, 1961, p. 561.

[2] Robert W. Campbell, "A Comparison of Soviet and American Inventory-Output Ratios," *American Economic Review,* Sept., 1958, p. 549.

ever, not only did the growth rate decline, it became evident that the wrong goods were being produced. The reformers soon began to realize that the Soviet system was not equipped to handle the changes in the needs and tastes of the customers. In the words of O. K. Antonov, the great Soviet aircraft designer, the Soviet system lacked feedback, or give and take between producers and consumers.[3] Since the Soviet producer had to answer to the plan, not to the customer, the factory and store managers had no reason to concern themselves with consumer tastes or quality. In effect, the goals of society and the goals of the manager were no longer the same. From the country's point of view, production for production's sake had lost its meaning. Inventories began to pile up. The warehouses were stuffed with more than $3 billion of goods above and beyond the normal inventory needs. Inventory accumulation of consumer goods was especially serious, but heavy industry products were also affected. Still, not many factory managers lost any sleep over this. Their task was to produce. Nevertheless, the economic reformers and a few state planners sat back and watched in horror. In the words of V. Dymshits, then chairman of the USSR Economic Council (Sovnarkhoz), "The time for striving for quantity at the expense of quality has passed." But as with the sorcerer's apprentice, there seemed to be no way to turn off the flood.

The changes that were taking place in the consumer sector were especially interesting for what they reveal about difficulties of planning in a country that is completing its process of industrialization. For almost 40 years, the Soviet economists were technically correct in their assertion that the Soviet system was a planned economy. Whatever they produced for the consumer was sold. Because so much was being invested in heavy industry and almost as much was being diverted to the governmental sector, there always seemed to be a shortage of resources available to satisfy the purchasing power of the consumers. Consequently, whatever was put on the store shelves was grabbed up quickly. The Soviet consumer simply could not afford to be particular. For many years, repressed inflation was a persistent curse. For the retailer, however, it was also a blessing.

By the late 1950s, supply conditions began to change. As incomes

[3] *Izvestiia*, May 25, 1962, p. 3. See also his book *Dlia Vsekh I Dlia Sebia*, Moscow, Ekonomika, 1965.

120

continued to rise, Soviet consumers began to find that it was no longer so difficult to find and buy the basic necessities of life. In fact, after they purchased their food and clothing, there were still goods on the shelves and money in their pockets. As we saw in Table 4, as production increased, much of this excess money went for the purchase of consumer durables. Production and sales went up at a phenomenal speed. But, as might be expected, there were limits to what could be purchased. One limit was the space in which most Russians had to put their purchases. Although material conditions improve each day, the majority of Russians still have no more than one or two rooms in their apartments. Thus there are few Russians who can be expected to buy two television sets or refrigerators. Moreover, because of the reluctance of Soviet manufacturers to innovate, there has not been much in the way of model change to whet the consumer's appetite. Consequently, there is seldom any reason to buy a new model; for a long time there have been no new models to buy.

As the standard of living was raised, the consumer's tastes also changed. One of the by-products of this change was that the Russian housewife began to buy more ready-to-wear clothing instead of buying a sewing machine to sew the fabrics herself. This should have been anticipated, but it was not. Ultimately, this tendency was recognized by the Soviet planners, but, as recently as 1961, it was planned that each Soviet home should have a sewing machine by 1980.[4] As indicated in Table 5, the Russians appear to have set a much lower target recently. The number of families with sewing machines is scheduled to rise from 52 per cent in 1965 to only 56 per cent by 1970. However, until the planners realized what was happening, the change in tastes had a disastrous impact on the sale and eventually the production of sewing machines. Sales fell off as early as 1961. Yet, production was not reduced until 1963. As indicated in Table 4, production was then slashed sharply so that, by 1964, production was only 1.6 million units compared with 3.3 million in 1962. In the meantime inventories grew at a frightening pace. Since the late 1950s, products such as bicycles, watches, radios, vacuum cleaners, motor scooters, cameras, and electric irons have been similarly affected by at least a temporary drop in either sales or production. Although

[4] *Sovetskaia Torgovlia*, Nov., 1961, p. 10.

camera and sewing machine sales and production have apparently dropped sharply since the early 1960's (in 1965 production of sewing machines was reduced to just about half of what it had been the year before), the sale and production of these as well as most other items have recovered after the drop. It is apparent from some of the complaints of the planners, however, that they have not always anticipated this either. The Russians have found themselves confronted with sales and production cycles, but their lack of feedback makes it impossible for them to respond in anything but a clumsy fashion. For example, because of a rapid expansion in the production of electric irons, the Russians were able to produce 5.3 million units in 1955. Unfortunately, this outpouring of irons flooded the market and eventually the warehouses. Consequently, in 1957, production was cut back to 1.7 million units. This over-response by the planners induced a shortage so that, by 1960, production was again increased to 5.3 million.[5]

Part of the reason for fluctuations of this sort is that the consumers suddenly find themselves with discretionary income. They have moved beyond the stage of subsistence and no longer must spend all their money on food. Once they have bought a variety of appliances, there is not much more they can buy until there is either more innovation or until they are able to move into a larger dwelling. Although only a few Soviet economists seem to be aware of the concept, the best way to explain what is happening is to say that the marginal propensity to consume in the Soviet Union has been falling. As illustrated in Table 6, each year since 1958, savings bank deposits have risen faster than sales. Although it was an unprecedented increase, savings grew by $4.6 billion in 1966. This was equal to one-half the growth in sales. Savings have also increased at a faster rate than incomes. This situation creates a whole new set of quandaries for the planner. He never knows when the consumer will choose to spend his savings and extra income. No longer is it safe to assume that whatever is produced will be sold. Furthermore, disruptions in the consumer goods sector are being accompanied by similar disruptions in heavy industry. Industrial buyers have started to reject unsuitable or poor quality products. Planning and production must be handled with much more sophistication and responsiveness if the Russians hope

[5] Marshall I. Goldman, "The Reluctant Consumer and Economic Fluctuations in the Soviet Union," *Journal of Political Economy*, Aug., 1965, p. 378.

TABLE 6 RELATION OF SALES, SAVINGS-BANK DEPOSITS, AND INVENTORY
(billions of rubles)
As of December 31, each year

Year	Sales (1)	Sales Increase (rubles) (2)	Sales Increase (per cent) (3)	Savings-Bank Deposits (4)	Increase in Savings-Bank Deposits (rubles) (5)	Increase in Savings-Bank Deposits (per cent) (6)	Retail and Wholesale Inventory (7)	Inventory Increase (per cent) (8)
1958	67.7	5.2	8.4	8.719	0.661	8.2	19.9	27
1959	71.9	4.2	6.2	10.056	1.337	15.3	23.1	16
1960	78.6	6.6	9.2	10.909	0.853	8.5	24.0	4
1961	81.1	2.5	3.2	11.671	0.762	7.0	26.2	9
1962	87.3	6.1	7.6	12.745	1.074	9.2	28.3	8
1963	91.6	4.3	5.0	13.945	1.247	9.8	30.8	9
1964	96.4	4.8	5.2	15.707	1.715	12.3	33.3	8
1965	103.5	7.1	7.3	18.727	3.020	19.2	34.9	5
1966	111.7	8.2	7.9	22.9	4.2	22.0		

Column
Sources: (1) *Nar. Khoz.,* 1965, p. 631; *Pravda,* Jan. 29, 1967, p. 2.
(4) *Nar. Khoz.,* 1961, p. 607; 1963, p. 508; 1965, p. 600; *Pravda,* Jan. 29, 1967, p. 2.
(7) *Nar. Khoz.,* 1965, p. 639.

to avoid growing waste, continuing confusion, and ever-increasing stocks of inventory.

The Proposal for Reforms

Suggestions about how to handle these accumulating problems had been offered for many years. However, in late 1962, a national debate took place in response to what seemed to many Americans as well as to many Russians to be the radical suggestions of Professor Evsei Liberman. Although his proposals were quite complicated, his most striking suggestion was that the system of physical targets be scrapped. In its place, he suggested that profits be used as the main determinant of enterprise and manager effectiveness. This meant that bonuses would be paid if the enterprise met the planned rate of return on capital, not its output plan. Liberman defined the rate of return as the ratio of profits over both the fixed and working capital of the enterprise. The manager himself would project his own rate of return for the plan period. Liberman sought to make the manager set his rate of return as high as possible. He thought this could be done if there was less emphasis on overfulfillment and more on fulfillment. Therefore, he urged that high premiums be paid for plan fulfillment but low premium rates be paid for overfulfillment. In this way, Liberman argued there would be less bargaining by the managers for low targets and also less storming to overfulfill the target.

The debate that followed upon Liberman's suggestions was surprisingly temperate in tone and serious in purpose. The last economic debate of any substance occurred in the 1920s over the future pattern of Soviet economic growth. Stalin eventually resolved that debate by declaring what he thought to be the solution and then jailing or executing all his opponents. This took much of the enthusiasm out of those economists who survived. Thereafter there was little widespread discussion. In fact, economists tended to be very reticent until the 1960s when Liberman's proposals were suddenly given prominence in *Pravda,* which connoted official sanction. Then economists and plant directors from all over the country joined in the discussion.

After almost two years of debate, the first substantial experiments

124

at reform were approved in May, 1964, when it was announced that a new planning system would be introduced in two textile factories, Bolshevichka in Moscow and Maiak in Gorky. They did not follow explicitly the Liberman proposals, but there were many similarities. Moreover, Liberman was brought in as a consultant to the All Union *Sovnarkhoz,* or Economic Council which was in charge of carrying on the experiment. The experiment differed from Liberman's original proposal in that profit was not made the sole success indicator. Instead, there were two major targets, profits and sales. In any case, enterprise bonuses were no longer tied to output targets. However, omitted from this experiment was any concern for promoting greater economy in the use of capital, which was so important in Liberman's original proposal. There was no rate of return calculation nor any other device to indicate that capital was a valuable commodity. Furthermore, nothing was done to encourage the establishment of high target rates initially which would thereby discourage efforts to set targets low in order to overfulfill the plan.

Gradually more and more firms were included in the new system. Suddenly, in the middle of the experiment, Khrushchev was removed from power. The experiment nonetheless continued. If anything, the whole movement gained momentum under the sponsorship of the new premier, Alexei Kosygin. In September, 1965, Kosygin declared that his government had been so pleased with the results that a revised version of the experiment would soon be adopted throughout the whole economy. As of January 1, 1966, 43 factories were converted to the new system, but it was declared that all of Soviet industry would be affected by the end of 1968.

As Kosygin's program unfolded, it looked more and more like Liberman's original proposal. The use of output targets was abandoned. In its place, a target for rate of return was added. This was something that Liberman had urged from the beginning since it forced plant managers to stress the economical use of capital. There was also a second target. Just as in the Bolshevichka and Maiak experiment of 1964, some enterprises were assigned a profit plan; alternatively other firms were required to meet a sales plan. This took the place of the profit plan, although profits continued to be important since they were a partial determinant of the rate of return. The sales plan was substituted for the profit plan in those enterprises where delivery of their output was considered a more crucial matter than the efficiency of their operations. The use of the sales plan ensured that the enterprise would only be given credit for goods actually delivered and paid for by the customer. As opposed to past practices, it would no longer be enough to manufacture the goods (they might end up in the warehouse) or ship them (they might not be accepted); there had to be an actual acceptance of the goods by the firms. This meant the manufacturers for the first time had to worry about quality and suitability. In all cases, however, the enterprises were evaluated by the rate of return they could achieve. Kosygin also restored Liberman's emphasis on setting the initial plan targets high. Bonuses for overfulfillment of the sales or profit plan were awarded at a lower rate than premiums for plan fulfillment. Consequently, managers suddenly found it more in their interest to set their sights high if they wanted to earn a high bonus.

Underlying the whole scheme is the desire to provide the enterprise manager with more power. By providing him with more discretion over his own activities and by removing what the Russians had come to call "petty tutelage," it was hoped that the manager would no longer worry about how to beat his target. Presumably, the manager could now concentrate on producing a needed product at a low cost. In other words, this was an attempt to redesign the incentive system so that once again it took advantage of the manager's momentum and fashioned his efforts to fit the purposes of the country.

Some of the other aspects of the reform focused on some of the other shortcomings of the old system. The manager was given more discretion over his labor force. Although he is still prohibited from firing workers without cause and he must continue to work closely with the trade union in juggling his labor force around, he can decide for himself how many people he wants to put in a specific job class. Before, this was all decided for him. The manager still is assigned a fixed wage fund which he cannot exceed, but, within that limit, he can adjust his work force. In 1966, some factories on the new system actually reduced the size of their work forces. Together, all the firms were utilizing an average of 0.8 per cent workers fewer than had been planned.[6] This meant that worker productivity had

⁶ N. Federenko, *Planovoe Khoziaistvo*, Apr., 1967, p. 8.

been increased more than anticipated. This also meant that there were fewer employees to share the bonuses. Although the bulk of the premiums earned because of higher profits were intended for the white-collar workers and managerial staff, the managers were also to share some with the blue-collar workers. In this way everyone stood to benefit.

One of the most surprising aspects of the reform was the candid recognition of the role of capital. We have seen the numerous distortions the failure to acknowledge the scarcity of capital has created in the past. Now, not only was the rate of return made a determinant of premiums, but Kosygin took the bull by at least one horn and introduced an explicit charge for capital. It would have been even better if he had taken both horns and called it openly "an interest charge," but even a capital charge is something that few observers thought they would ever see in the USSR. Each firm must now pay to the government an amount equivalent to about 6 per cent of the value of the enterprise's fixed and working capital. The rate varies among firms, but 6 per cent is the average. Moreover, Gosbank must charge an interest rate on long-term loans. The interest rates are still quite low, but, until 1966, there were no interest rates on long-term loans and, for the most part, there were no loans. Previously long-term capital was provided almost solely in grant form. As a result, there was no concern about repayment.

Almost of equal surprise was the introduction of a charge for rent. This was intended primarily for mining and other activities where there are important natural differences due either to quality or location. Perhaps of all the changes, the introduction of a capital charge (or interest) and rent are the most radical. After all, the concept of profit had been used in the Soviet economy for a long time. Therefore, making profit the main determinant of enterprise activity was unexpected but not heretical. The use of interest and rent goes far beyond the ideological bounds and is a frank obeisance to the pragmatic needs of an industrialized society.

The reform also involved several other measures which seemed to move it away from the strict confines of centralized planning. Soviet economists now talk of ultimately permitting and even encouraging firms to make direct contracts with one another instead of requiring them to negotiate through intermediary agencies in their Ministry or

Gosplan. This would reduce the scope of physical planning and the direct allocation of goods. The Russians apparently will maintain the physical allocation of certain priority products, but, wherever possible, they apparently intend to encourage independent initiative by the enterprise. Toward this end, Kosygin announced at the time of the reform that a new All Union Committee for Material and Technical Supply would be formed. Some interpreted this as just another bureaucratic device to clutter up the distribution process. But this does not appear to be the intention of the official in charge of this new ministry. He is V. E. Dymshits, who was the same man in charge of the All Union Sovnarkhoz when it sponsored the initial experiment with the Bolshevichka and Maiak plants.

Dymshits and his subordinates have gone far out of their way to indicate that they see their function to be the elimination rather than the perpetuation of red tape. They are busily involved in establishing a series of large wholesale warehouses across the country. As opposed to past practice, these warehouses contain the products of many ministries, not just those of a specific ministry or agency. The best analogy for an American is that the new warehouses will operate in much the same way as a wholesale supplier of automobile parts does in the United States. They stock parts from a variety of manufacturers from all over the country. The purpose of such warehouses is to centralize the supplies of many producers so they are conveniently available for many users. In this way, there is no need for each manufacturer to hoard his own little treasure chest of supplies. Once everyone sees that the supplies he needs are readily available, there will be no reason to hoard.

Dymshits' organization has made considerable progress. By early 1967, more than 1000 goods including more than 100 oil products were distributed this way.[7] Another innovation is the creation of somewhat smaller wholesale stores. There were 120 of these stores in May of 1967, and it was planned to double their number to 240 by the end of the year. These stores sell freely to purchasers from other factories. For the most part they carry miscellaneous supplies, but the intention is to provide flexibility in the procurement of small items

[7] V. Kurotchenko, *Material'no-Technicheskoe Snabzhenie*, Mar., 1967, pp. 90-95.

that previously had to be anticipated in a plan drawn up as much as a year and a half in advance of need.[8]

Another technique being used by the new Committee is the trade fair or *iamarka*. As in the West, the purpose of these fairs is to bring buyers and sellers together at the beginning of the season to demonstrate the new product line and to sign up customers. This helps to guide manufacturers as to exactly what they should produce, and it helps the customers determine who is making what. It also eliminates much of the difficulty that used to exist in matching buyers and sellers together within the offices of Gosplan. It obviously is more efficient when the buyers and sellers reach an agreement by themselves. In 1966, 57 such fairs were held. These fairs also provide an ideal way for selling not only new products but surplus stocks that have accumulated for one reason or another. More than $800 million worth of surplus stocks were put back into circulation in this way in 1966.

The ultimate impact of the new ministry is indicated by the assertion that "the directions for the 1966-70 Five-Year Plan call for the gradual replacement of the planned distribution of the means of production by wholesale trade." [9] Certainly this is a far-reaching statement. But as the Soviet economist A. Birman put it, "only three years ago, no one would have thought that there would be anything but Funds (the direct physical allocation of goods). Now economists talk of trading (*torgovat*) instead of allocating (*snabzhat*)." [10]

Equally significant for its impact on the trend toward decentralization is the increased power given to the manager to allocate capital. In a marked departure from past practice, factory managers should soon be able to decide for themselves how to allocate 20 per cent of the country's investment. Heretofore, almost all capital investment has been determined centrally. The reform provided that each firm should have its own Development Fund. Revenue for this Fund is provided by diverting 30 to 50 per cent of the firm's normal depreciation charges plus a specified sum from the enterprise's profits. Thus increased profits now serve not only as a source of higher premiums but also of more investment for the firm. This should provide double incentive for the manager to maximize his profits.

[8] *Ekonomicheskaia Gazeta,* No. 18 (May, 1967), p. 7.
[9] *Material'no-Technicheskoe Snabzhenie,* Dec., 1966, pp. 33-37.
[10] *Novyi Mir,* Jan., 1967, p. 170.

The purpose of creating something like the Development Fund fits into the general pattern of the reform. Although there is no desire to eliminate the role of the state as a guiding force in the economy, there is the realization that the central authorities cannot oversee every decision as they used to when the economy was younger and more easily managed from one location. There are some decisions that the manager on the spot, even a bad manager, can make better than even a good planner in Moscow. The Yugoslavs have gone to the other extreme and decentralized about 70 per cent of their capital investment decisions. The Russians are likely to go much slower, but the purpose of the change is the same in both countries.

There is another advantage to decentralizing the allocation of capital. By making it possible for the enterprise manager to plan some of his own investment, the reformers hope there will be more product and performance innovation. In the past, whenever he had a new idea, the manager had to fight with all kinds of senior officials before he could obtain the funds to implement his proposal. Usually, it was not worth the effort. Now this is no longer necessary. Hopefully, the manager will be able to pursue new ideas without checking everything first in Moscow.

The reformers made the changes which they hoped would encourage the spirit and risk of innovation. The targets for profits, sales, and rate of return are now set several years in advance. In this way the engineers and enterprise managers no longer need to worry that, if they improve efficiency, all the fruits of their efforts will be taxed away by jacking up the norms. This was inevitably what happened before. Therefore, some enterprises may now take the risk of losing some money the first year or so while they perfect a new product in exchange for the expectation of considerably higher profits in later years. These higher profits will not all be drawn off by the state. Instead, they can be used for profit sharing and the capital Development Fund. Thus no longer need the white-collar workers and the managers be reluctant to tinker with new ideas because they might jeopardize the fulfillment of the output plan and thus their premium. Now, in exchange for innovation, the manager and his engineers may earn considerably higher salaries. Probably it is too much to expect that every manager or engineer will accept the challenge (certainly not every manager accepts the risk in this country), but the reformers feel that conditions will be no worse than they have been in the past and hopefully a lot better.

Price Reforms

All of these measures, especially the emphasis on profits, will only be meaningful and bring about improved rationality if the managers are made to respond to the right signals. The restoration of interest and rent is an important step in the right direction. But it should be readily apparent that, if prices do not reflect economic costs properly or do not establish some kind of equilibrating balance between producers and customers (suppliers and demanders), then profits will be made by producing the wrong kind of goods. Moreover, because of the major disproportions that have been built into the economy in the past, a sudden transition to a decentralized form of decision making would create a serious disruption of economic activity. There was justifiable fear that Soviet managers would discover that enormous profits could be made by catering to pent-up consumer demands. This might generate a radical reorientation of productive effort. Certainly it would mean a down-grading of heavy industry.

Because there has been no major price revision in the USSR for more than ten years, Soviet economists were keenly aware of the serious disruption of economic activity that might result unless there was an accompanying adjustment of the price structure. Even if it is assumed that the last price readjustment in 1955 was a good one, it would not take much to prove that relative costs and demand conditions have changed significantly in the interim. Unless prices were adjusted to take these altered relationships into consideration, managers would only produce goods when their prices were unduly high. It was a matter of top priority, therefore, to have a price reform. Just such a major revision was made on July 1, 1967. With a sweep that caught most Western observers unprepared, the Russians acted as if they fully realized how seriously their price structure needed revision. Price changes were especially significant in industries which had been heavily subsidized in the past. For example, the wholesale price of coal (a key commodity) was raised by 78 per cent, and the price of oil was increased to 2.3 times its former level. Revisions almost as fundamental were made in other basic products such as rolled metals, where prices were increased by 43 per cent.[11]

Despite the magnitude of some of the changes and the formal recognition of a capital charge and rent, observers of the Soviet scene as well as Soviet authorities themselves have expressed considerable doubt that all of these changes can be successfully implemented without a prolonged series of subsequent readjustments. Since prices and costs are interrelated, it is hard to know what the price of steel should be until it is known what the price of coal is; but, in turn, you must know the price of steel to set the price of coal. All of this suggests how complicated such a reform can be. Nonetheless, it is still impressive that the Russians have moved as far as they have.

Marketing

Along with the recognition that production operations and motivations must be reorganized, the reformers have also turned their attention to some of the marketing or commercial aspects of the problem. To the outside observer, it has long been clear that Soviet economic problems do not stem solely from difficulties in the production sector. Undoubtedly, a more responsive productive mechanism will eliminate much of the damage, but one of the things the Russians have been slow to understand is that an efficient marketing sector provides the productive sector with extra room for maneuvering. In other words, regardless of what Marx or the Russians might claim about the omniscience of their planners, it is impossible to make provision for every variation in human or physical events. Consequently, there are bound to be shortages and surpluses, but, supported by a good marketing ensemble, the surpluses can be much more easily disposed of and shortages solved by diverting customers to some other product. The marketing agencies of course can also create their own needs and generate their own problems. Although we often overreact to the shortcomings of such institutions, we forget that they do facilitate the smooth operation of the productive sector.

[11] *Ekonomicheskaia Gazeta,* **27,** July, 1967, p. 10.

Because Marx so often regarded anything other than production as a parasitic activity, the Russians have long had an aversion to anything vaguely connected with marketing. Only when it came to be realized that some marketing techniques would indeed have to be adopted if the production process was to be improved, did ideological attitudes change. Although it is almost impossible to find any ideological justification for it in Marx, the Russians now openly approve of the formation of Soviet advertising agencies and the training of advertising specialists. Actually, the first agencies were formed in the late 1950s when, as we saw, surplus stocks became a real problem. Recently, however, advertising has been given renewed emphasis. All-Socialist advertising conferences have been held with regularity, and contests are held each year to determine the best display windows and promotional designs.

Market research has been raised onto a similar pedestal. As long as there were shortages of goods, no one had to worry about consumer tastes or desires. Whenever they saw a queue, many Russians automatically stopped whatever they were doing and joined the line. But we noted how this situation had changed. By 1965, the heretofore uncoordinated efforts at market research were accorded official sanction, and an all-union marketing research organization was established with branches in the various republics.

There is considerable discussion as to just what the function of such groups should be. Some Soviet economists argue that scientific norms should be established and studies made to determine just how close present consumption patterns correspond to these norms. The decision that every family should have a sewing machine by 1980 whether it wanted one or not reflected this kind of thinking. Such an attitude brings to mind the story of the party agitator who was vividly depicting the glories of Communism to a group of poor peasants before the revolution. At the climax to his speech he exclaimed, "Comes the Revolution, Comrades, everyone will eat strawberries and cream!" Amid the cheering that followed, a little peasant raised his hand in the back of the room with a question. "But, Comrade, what happens if I don't like strawberries and cream?" The speaker frowned and quickly replied, "Comes the Revolution, Comrade, you will eat strawberries and cream and like it!"

A somewhat different kind of approach involves less prescribing

133

and more analyzing. Other Soviet economists are not so much concerned about what the Soviet consumer should have but about what the consumer selects as his income increases and prices change. This approach is similar to the type of demand analysis conducted in the West.

One sign that market research has finally been given official status is that the market researchers have also held an All-Socialist conference. The first International Conference on Techniques of Demand Analysis was held in July, 1967. Marketing research in the USSR, like advertising, has come of age.

Another device which has become very popular in the USSR is installment credit. Since it was first introduced in 1960, the volume of goods sold on credit has risen steadily to over $3.7 billion by 1965, or slightly more than 7 per cent of all the nonfood goods sold.[12] This growth has taken place despite the fact that peasants are not eligible for credit. For some Russian Marxists, installment credit has been one of the more difficult measures to accept. For a long time, party officials persisted in calling installment credit nothing but a tool for impoverishing the workers in a capitalist society. After all, even the harshest critics of interest had always taken a dimmer view of interest for consumer borrowing than interest for productive purposes. Then, with barely a pause to correct the official party textbooks, installment credit was made available in the USSR. Of course, installment credit had to wait until there were surplus stocks of appliances which had to be cleared from the shelves. But, once it was realized that installment credit, like advertising and market research, could be used to relieve pressures in the productive sphere, then it too became ideologically acceptable.

Business Administration

The task of administering Soviet enterprises in this brave new world is obviously not the same as it used to be. For this, a whole new breed of administrators must be prepared. Clearly, it will no longer do to

[12] *Nar. Khoz., 1965,* p. 634.

train enterprise managers who take their Marxism literally. Instead, the Russians will have to seek managers who worry about satisfying customers and their changing needs instead of favoring planners and their output targets. This will not be an easy thing to do. After all, there are no business schools in the USSR, and those presently in charge cannot be used to set the example for future managers since the present managers are products of the old system.

Some steps are being taken to correct the situation. Suggestions are being made that business schools on the pattern of the Harvard Business School should be established in the USSR. During the school year of 1966 to 1967, a Russian attended Harvard Business School to study the case-study method and see what techniques of teaching business administration might be worth transplanting to the USSR. Such training will have immediate use. Many factories operating under the new reform have already taken the opportunity to create the position of Commercial Manager. The Commercial Manager will rank second in command under the Enterprise Manager, and his job will be to ensure the sale of the enterprise's goods and anticipate future production requirements. This may be taken as a sign of the times. Previously, the second in command was the Chief Engineer, whose function was to ensure that the production targets were fulfilled. Now the Chief Engineer shares his command position with the Commercial Manager. Some Soviet economists have even gone so far as to call for the rehabilitation of the position of *kommersant*. Literally translated, this means a merchant or businessman.[13] This throwback to prerevolutionary terminology may cause confusion among the seekers of ideological truth, but it more accurately reflects the pragmatic needs of the economy.

REALITY: *From the beginning, the Soviet government disregarded the teachings of Marxist ideology whenever they found that certain institutions were essential for the operation of the economy. Some tools of capitalism were discarded occasionally because of "principle," but just as often these tools were considered an obstacle to rapid economic development. As the country*

[13] *Sovetskaia Torgovlia,* June, 1967, p. 24.

became more and more industrialized, more and more problems developed which seemed to be incurable under existing modes of operation. Increasingly, the Russians found their problems to be ever more similar to those in other industrialized countries. Consequently, with slight regard for ideological principles, the Soviet government in 1965 decided to move away from the system of centrally planned determination and allocation of goods. To do this meant providing the manager with more control over his own operation, which in turn meant providing him with guidance and motivational tools such as interest, rent, profit sharing, decentralized capital investment, advertising, market research, and installment credit.

CHAPTER 10

MYTH: *The Soviet Union is becoming capitalist, and, in a few years, there will be no differences between the Soviet and American economic systems.*

The new leaders of the Soviet Communist Party are leading the Soviet Union down the path of capitalism in the name of "realizing communism." . . . Through a party resolution and government decrees, the new leaders of the Russian Communist Party have confirmed the experiments initiated in the Khrushchev period. As a result, socialist enterprises owned by all the people have degenerated into enterprises of a capitalist nature and they have spread these enterprises throughout the country. The key feature of the "new system" of industrial management is to enforce the capitalist principle of profit and to make profit-seeking the basic motive force of production in the enterprises through the "enhancement of economic incentives." In the name of widening the enterprises' right to self-management, they have scrapped a series of important quotas formerly set by the state for the enterprise in accordance with the plan, substituting free competition for socialist planned economy. They have vested in the manager the power to hire and fire workers, fix the level of wages and bonuses, and freely dispose of large capital funds, thus turning the managers into virtual masters of their workers. In reality this means restoring capitalism, replacing socialist ownership by all the people with ownership by the privileged bourgeois stratum and converting socialist enterprises in the Soviet Union step by step into capitalist enterprises of a special type.

The rather lengthy statement quoted above illustrates that, as there are those who see the Soviet Union as the realization of the Marxist dream, so others argue that the Soviet economic system is barely distinguishable from the traditional economic system of capitalism. The feeling of growing convergence has been especially strong in the West. Ironically, however, the preceding quotation is not that of a Western observer, but of the Communist Chinese newspaper, *Red Flag,* of November 11, 1965.

For their own reasons, the Chinese have taken a special delight in taunting the Soviet Union about its economic reforms. From the Russian point of view, however, there is just enough truth in what the Chinese say to make the Russians very defensive and nervous. Still, it seems reasonable to predict that, even though the Russians will adopt more and more of the forms in use in other advanced industrial countries, this will not make them capitalistic in the American sense. In our discussion before, we saw how all heavily capitalized countries have many of the same problems to solve. Inevitably they seem to find it expedient to use the same type of tools to cope with these problems. It is safe to say, however, that the Russians will retain ownership of the means of production in the hands of the state. As long as there is no complete breakdown of the economy nor a depression, it is unlikely that the keys to heavy industrial plants will be turned over to private owners. That would involve a complete rejection of the revolution, and the country would probably have to be on the verge of collapse before that would happen.

Conceivably, the Russians will ultimately decide to permit some private ownership in service industries, where fewer than perhaps five or ten employees are involved. The Yugoslavs have long permitted such activities, and now the Poles, Czechs, and Hungarians seem to be moving in the same direction. The rationale for this throwback to bourgeois habits is that there is no other way to provide services for the consumer in a cheap and efficient manner. Such small activities will not threaten the state's control of the economy, and, at the same time, it will make for more flexibility. Certainly, there is room for it.

The problem of private traders and craftsmen will be more acute in the Soviet Union in the years ahead. The automotive age seems to spawn private enterprise at least on a small scale. Because it is such a complex instrument, automobiles are always in need of repair.

Because service is usually difficult to obtain from authorized repair shops (even in this country), it is only natural that the car owner should turn for help to anyone with mechanical training regardless of whether the mechanic has been officially authorized by the state to accept such work. (The same thing is likely to happen to workers trained as electricians, plumbers, and carpenters.) Eventually, part-time work could be more lucrative than the full-time job.

Not only does the automobile generate its own demand for services, it also makes it easier to supply services. In our country, the automobile is a producer's good as well as a consumer's good. The car is useful to other producers and businessmen in addition to the more commonly thought of traveling salesmen. It can serve as a traveling workbench for the plumbers, painters, electricians, and carpenters who would otherwise find it hard to lug all their equipment around through the subways. In other words, as more and more automobiles are produced, more and more artisans will be able to expand their range of activities. It would seem to be good sense to encourage them to do so.

There are many in the USSR who agree with the Chinese and oppose the whole trend of events. Opposition has been especially strong in the Ministry of Finance. They see the state losing control over its own destiny. Some economists have expressed open fears that Soviet managers will come to shun unprofitable projects which may nonetheless be valuable from the national point of view. For example, Soviet showpieces such as their subway system, their great dams, and their massive housing program might never have been undertaken without substantial government subsidies. In a sense these critics take the position of some American economists who also worry over what John Kenneth Galbraith calls "social imbalance" in this country. While Galbraith argues that the state should assume more control at the expense of the individual enterprise in economic affairs, the Soviet opponents of the reform pull from the other side and argue that the state should not yield its control.

Few Soviet officials pretend that implementation of the reform will be easy. Kosygin himself warned the Supreme Soviet that there was considerable bureaucratic opposition. Like bureaucrats anyplace in the world, to some Soviet officials change is always a threat. Undoubtedly, some jobs will be lost and some empires will crumble. In fact, the very purpose of the reform is to destroy bureaucratic empires. Therefore, it was not entirely unexpected that Kosygin should find that "a certain conservatism and lack of initiative are sometimes displayed in trying to solve a number of matters connected with the operation of the economic reforms." Several ministries have refused to adjust to the new conditions and persist in their old ways. As Kosygin put it, "The Ministries should not demand an excessive amount of reference notes and information of various kinds from the enterprise." Continual interference by the Ministries defeats the purpose of the whole thing.

The bureaucrats are not of course the only ones who fear the reform. Like their counterparts all over the world, many Soviet managers fear the effects of open competition and are reluctant to forsake the relatively tranquil climate of fixed markets and stable production quotas which they have become accustomed to over the years. Moreover, like the workers in Alec Guiness's movie, *The Man in the White Suit,* there are many Soviet workers who realize that increased efficiency will imperil their jobs and might mean layoffs or unemployment.

The supporters of the reform recognize some of these dangers but argue that progress cannot be attained in any other way. Furthermore, they assert that adoption of the reform will not mean a complete surrender to the spontaneous forces of the market. Quite the contrary, they say; no longer will the authorities in Moscow have to worry about such things as whether a factory in Minsk is sending the right size screw to the right factory in Pinsk on time or how many workers should be assigned to picking up trash. Once they are freed of such chores, they will be able to focus instead on larger issues such as what new forms of transportation will be needed, where should new industries be located, and what new products should be provided capital for financing. Where necessary, heavy industry can still be protected by the use of price adjustments and government subsidies.

If the above analysis is correct, it may be that some day the Chinese will find themselves undergoing the same type of reforms. In a sense, it is easy for them to throw criticisms now because their own economy is in such an underdeveloped state. It will be fascinating to see if their tone changes as their economy changes.

It will not be because they have come to agree with Chinese criticism, but it is nonetheless likely that the Russians will hesitate a little and perhaps abandon some of their reforms. This is only to be expected. The Soviet experiment brings to mind the secret of the success of a Boston business consultant. The first thing he does when analyzing the problems of a troubled corporation is to ask for the corporation's table of organization. If the firm is centralized he sends in his bill with the recommendation that the corporation decentralize. If the firm is decentralized, he sends in his bill with the recommendation that the firm centralize. Liberman has prescribed a strong dose of decentralization for an overly centralized system which found itself with an inappropriate and outdated system of goals. It would not be surprising if his successors some day find themselves prescribing at least a bit of the opposite medicine. Whatever the backtracking, however, the Russians seem to be beyond the point of returning to the system they once knew. The Russians are intent on improving the effectiveness of a form of state capitalism. The dynamic operations of a massive and complex industrial system compels the use of certain universal techniques. The Russians actually do not have too much choice; it is like trying to go up the down escalator. As their economy becomes more complicated, it becomes harder and harder to move forward at a rapid rate. Without the reform, their economy might well have been carried backward. With the reform they hope to resume their march forward.

REALITY: *The Soviet Union is not turning capitalist in the usual sense of the word. It is unlikely that private ownership of the means of production will ever be tolerated, except perhaps in a few small service industries or trades. Still, because Russia is a heavily capitalized state, the task of coordinating and administrating an ever more complex organism is facilitated by the use of certain economic mechanisms and techniques. In fact there seems to be general agreement that without such phenomena as interest, rent, credit, money, and a profit incentive, or some such surrogates, there will be economic irrationality and excess. The introduction and approval of such devices does not herald the advent of private capitalism; rather, it indicates a determined effort to improve the effectiveness of a form of state capitalism.*

PART V

Foreign
Economic
Activity

CHAPTER 11

MYTH: *In contrast to the Western world, the Russians have never used foreign trade as an imperialist device to take advantage of other countries.*

As in almost all statements about the Soviet Union, there is a little bit of truth along with a variety of mistruth. In the case of Soviet involvement in the economic affairs of other countries, there is glory and shame.

Immediately after the Revolution, the Russians did renounce most of their interests in foreign countries. They unilaterally turned over their investments to the local governments and decided to cancel all debts owed to them. At the same time, of course, they also declared they would refuse to pay their debts to others, notably France and England. Although it was nice of the Russians to abandon their economic claims in places like Afghanistan and Turkey, the Russian debt to others was so large that this decision was received with something less than warm enthusiasm in the West. Naturally the Russians came out ahead since they owed considerably more to others than was owed to them.

Actually Soviet withdrawal from economic involvement in other countries was not complete. First of all, some of the more strident nationalists in the Central Asian and Caucasian regions of the Soviet Union argued violently that the Russians should also withdraw from their areas as well. However, Lenin insisted that annexation of these areas was not like Czarist imperialism but a natural expansion of

145

socialism and the Russian nation. He was not entirely consistent since Finland was given its independence. In any case, the force of Russian arms put an end to all the discussions. The Russians soon recognized, moreover, that some parts of their Czarist inheritance were too valuable to give up. In 1924, they reasserted their interest in the Chinese Eastern Railway. This railroad located on foreign territory had been a source of contention on the part of both China and Japan. The Russians maintained their interest in the railroad until 1935 when it looked as if the Japanese were about to confiscate the railroad for themselves anyway. Then they agreed to sell their share to the Japanese puppet state of Manchukuo. Although it meant ignoring their earlier moral protestations, the Russians did not appear to be unduly upset about accepting payment for a Czarist investment on foreign territory.

It was also in the 1920s that the Russians openly launched an economic invasion of the border state of Mongolia. Subsequently, of course, Mongolia became a close ally of the Soviet Union and a member of COMECON, the Council for Mutual Economic Assistance. (This is the economic coordinating and trade organization of the Communist countries of Eastern Europe, except Albania. Mongolia was included in 1962, as a slap in the face to its neighbor China.) By 1926, the Russians had virtually succeeded in excluding other foreign trade firms from Mongolia. This affected firms from China, the United States, and England. The Russians replaced them, not surprisingly, with their own trade firms.

The Russians then conceived of the idea of setting up Joint Stock Companies.[1] These groups were theoretically owned jointly by the Russians and the host country, but, in fact, effective control was exercised by the Russians. Ultimately, these Joint Stock Companies penetrated into almost every sector of the Mongolian economy. During World War II, the Mongolians were able to regain control of some of their own affairs. However, after the war, the Joint Stock Companies resumed much of their former influence. It was only in 1953 that the Russians began to close down some of the Joint Stock Companies. They proceeded however in a leisurely way until the late 1950s when

[1] Most of the material that follows was taken from Marshall I. Goldman, *Soviet Foreign Aid*. New York: Frederick A. Praeger, 1967, Chapters 1 and 2.

the Chinese began to shout about the Soviet Union's imperialistic role in Mongolia.

The Joint Stock Companies of Mongolia served as a pattern for the Joint Stock Companies the Russians were to set up in Eastern Europe and China. After World War II, the Allies awarded Russia possession of captured German assets not only in Germany but in all the East European countries. It often made little difference whether the property was in a country which had been a member of the Axis bloc or a country like Poland or Yugoslavia, both of which had been Allies in World War II. The Russians simply refused to entertain the idea that German property located in Poland should be Polish. The Poles were given this property only after they agreed to provide low-price coal to the USSR. The Russians themselves later conceded that they had underpaid the Poles by about $600 million. Furthermore, the Russians also claimed property which had originally been owned by the Allies and confiscated by the Germans only during the last days of the war.

The Joint Stock Companies in Europe were bitterly resented by the host countries. For the most part, the Russians contributed nothing but the captured German assets. To match this, the partner had to contribute assets of equal value. In effect the partner was financing both sides of the partnership because the property was all located on their territory. The Russians brought in little if anything from the USSR itself. In exchange for its contribution, the local country was allowed to nominate the president of the Joint Stock Companies. The Russians always magnanimously agreed that their representative would be nothing more than the director general. Of course, the president was always made a figurehead, and the director general took over actual control.

One of the key factors leading to the break between Yugoslavia and the USSR in 1948 was Yugoslav resentment over the Joint Stock Companies. When the Russians sought to create additional Joint Stock Companies, the Yugoslavs feared this would lead to the complete domination of their economy by the USSR, and they bitterly rejected Soviet demands. They later presented documentation to show how the Russians not only extracted 50 per cent of the profits of such companies for repatriation to the USSR, but how the Russians used the Joint Stock Companies in neighboring satellite countries to put the economic squeeze on Yugoslavia. For example, the Yugoslavs suddenly found they were unable to obtain raw materials such as oil from Rumanian Joint Stock Companies. In this way the Russians thought they could force Yugoslav adherence to Soviet demands. The Yugoslavs were equally bitter about the Russian attempt to form a shipping cartel on the Danube under the control of its solely-owned shipping company. This was very simple to arrange since all the director generals of all the Joint Stock Shipping Companies along the Danube were Russian and could agree to surrender their rights to the purely Soviet company. Although the Yugoslavs were the only ones to protest openly, and then only a few years after the attempt had been made, it is safe to assume that the other countries were equally disturbed.

If nothing else can be said for them, it is clear that the Russians had good business judgment. Wherever possible, they took control of the most valuable assets the country had to offer. In Bulgaria, they took over 90 per cent of the nonferrous metal enterprises; in Hungary, they took over the bauxite mines; and, in Rumania, they took over the oil. Reportedly, they also set up Joint Stock Companies in Czechoslovakia, Rumania, Hungary, and East Germany to operate uranium mines.

The Russians also set up Joint Stock Companies in China. They reasserted their control over the Chinese Eastern Railroad, now called the *Changchun Railroad,* and over Port Arthur, old Czarist possessions. Ironically, as long as the Nationalist Chinese were in power, the Russians were able to do no more. Only when the Communists took over in 1949 were the Russians able to win permission to set up four additional Joint Stock Companies. At least while Stalin was alive, it almost seems fair to conclude that the Russians felt less inhibition about exploiting fellow communist countries than they felt with non-communist countries. In a sense, the Russians seem to have regarded other Communist states as their own economic preserve.

This possessive attitude is also reflected in the pricing policies used by the Russians. Although the subject is a complicated one and has stirred up a good deal of controversy, there is evidence to indicate that the Russians used a form of discriminatory pricing in dealing with

148

their satellites at least until 1955.[2] The price paid for Polish coal is one of the more blatant examples. Similarly, any goods sold by the Joint Stock Companies to the USSR seemed to have been offered at reduced rates. Whatever the actual merits of the case, the satellite nations feel they were the victims of price exploitation.

Recognizing that the Joint Stock Companies were a deep source of bitterness, the Russians started gradually to dismantle them after the Berlin demonstration in 1953. At first they demanded compensation for what they said was their share of the investment. After the Hungarian and Polish uprisings in 1956, they decided to accelerate their withdrawal. The Joint Stock Companies were closed down, and the demands for compensation were withdrawn. At the same time, the Russians began their first significant help to their East European allies. After draining off resources for almost ten years in the form of either reparations, Joint Stock Companies, or discriminatory prices, the Russians agreed to provide substantial loans. It seems clear that the main stimulus for the loans was the realization that there would be more Polands and Hungaries if something was not done to right the economic balance within the Communist bloc. But for reasons that are still not clear, just as the resources began to flow to Eastern Europe, the Russians began to draw back on their promises of new loans to China. Actually China was the one country that had received significant Russian help before 1956. But in 1956 the Russians apparently began the curtailment of their aid to China which led to their abrupt withdrawal of foreign technicians in 1960. Russian aid support continued on a reduced scale after 1960, but the Russian actions in 1956 and 1960 created deep bitterness among the Chinese.

REALITY: *Despite their protestations, the Russians have been as guilty of economic exploitation as the most heartless imperialists in the West. Their attitudes have since changed considerably (are they copying the reforms of Standard Oil and United Fruit?), but, when provided with the opportunity, they grabbed like old professionals.*

[2] For a discussion of the issues, see Goldman, *Soviet Foreign Aid*, p. 5.

CHAPTER 12

MYTH: *When it comes to foreign trade it is impossible to compete on equal terms with the Russians. Because all foreign trade activities are monopolized in the hands of the state, it is impossible for private traders in a foreign country to command the resources and coordinate themselves as well as a state Ministry of Foreign Trade.*

For a time it did indeed appear that the Russians had developed a new supermethod of conducting foreign trade. Because they had the full strength of the state behind them, there seemed to be no limit to what they could do. With an astonishing sense for the dramatic, the Russians always seemed to pop out to support faltering markets. At the crucial moment, they agreed to buy Burma's rice, Egypt's cotton, Ghana's cocoa, Brazil's coffee, and Cuba's sugar. While American businessmen sat around wringing their hands and complaining that the independent businessman simply could not contend with such unequal competition, the Russians seemed to be sailing ahead, disrupting and soothing international markets at will.

After a time it became readily apparent that the Russians were not really that much better off after all. There were limits to the commodities that the USSR could buy. Like any other unit, the USSR found that it could only consume or store so much rice, cocoa, coffee, cotton, and sugar. Moreover, because the Soviet Union was a poorer country than the United States, there were fewer resources available to bolster up faltering markets.

The same kind of modification must be used to describe Soviet efforts at dumping. For a time some Western businessmen complained that the Russians were out to disrupt world markets wherever and whenever they could. Although there may have been such an intention at one time, the prime Soviet purpose recently has been to earn as much money as they could in world markets. Since most Western traders and governments discriminated against Soviet products with either higher tariffs or import quotas, the Russians found that they often had to cut prices to gain entry for their goods. As soon as possible, however, they tried to return prices to their higher levels. It soon became clear that the Russians had only a limited variety of products to sell. Most of their machinery and other fabricated goods were inferior in quality to Western products. Consequently the Russians found they had to divert most of their manufactured merchandise to the underdeveloped countries. Out of necessity, the Russians found that the only thing they could consistently sell to the Western countries was commodities. Thus the biggest exports of the Russians to Western Europe consist of lumber, paper products, oil, coal, and nonferrous metals.

With such a limited range of goods to offer, it comes as something of a surprise to find that the USSR actually has a very favorable balance of trade with her major trading partners in Western Europe as well as Japan. See Table 7. The Russians explain that they must build up such balances if they are going to accumulate enough to repay the long-term credits that companies and banks in these countries have been making to the USSR. Such arguments do not seem to satisfy Russia's trade partners. For example, England and France have openly complained that the Russians are not buying enough from them despite Russian calls for more trade. The moral here is that, despite the vastness of Soviet needs, there is not necessarily a pot of gold at the end of a Soviet trade agreement.

Despite the fact that Russian foreign trade is the monopoly of the Ministry of Foreign Trade, there does not always appear to be a co-ordinated trade policy. On occasion, American businessmen have reported that Russian officials will fight openly among themselves during trade negotiations. The people representing the factories argue for the high quality and high-priced imports. The people from the Ministry of Foreign Trade argue for cheaper imports and lower ex-

(millions of dollars)

	1958	1960	1962	1964	1965	1966
England						
Imports	145.5	148.9	161.0	111.2	128.6	141.1
Exports	166.5	209.8	235.5	252.9	333.0	351.8
France						
Imports	75.9	115.6	138.1	64.1	72.0	75.6
Exports	94.9	94.7	110.7	141.2	146.0	171.6
West Germany						
Imports	72.2	185.3	206.8	193.6	146.3	135.3
Exports	92.0	160.1	215.0	234.3	275.3	288.2
Italy						
Imports	31.1	78.6	102.3	90.7	98.1	90.1
Exports	40.4	125.8	166.3	147.2	181.3	190.0
Japan						
Imports	18.1	60.0	149.4	181.9	168.3	215.0
Exports	22.2	87.0	147.2	266.7	240.2	300.4

Source: Various issues of *Directions of Trade*, published by the International Monetary Fund and the International Bank for Reconstruction and Development.

penditure of foreign exchange. When negotiating over the possibility of an export sale, the positions are reversed with the factories concerned that, if the price is set too high, the deal will fall through.

There are of course still many instances when the Russians try to play off a manufacturer from one country against a manufacturer in another country. In this way, they are sometimes able to win a better price or credit concession. Occasionally, the competition for contracts in Eastern Europe is very intense. Reportedly one of the reasons that the Krupp Company in West Germany has had financial difficulties was that it offered credit to Eastern Europe on terms that were too liberal. The point to notice, however, is that the Western firm is not always the loser. Not only are Western firms and governments beginning to supply one another with more information about such attempts to win such concessions, but, as we have seen, the Russians themselves are not always able to coordinate their tactics or information well enough to take advantage of such possibilities. Surprisingly enough, one remedy that has already been adopted as part of the economic reforms in Eastern Europe and may also come to the USSR is the decision to allow the manufacturing enterprise itself to conduct its own foreign trade negotiations without interference from the Ministry of Trade. By allowing a few of the more important firms in Poland, Hungary, and Czechoslovakia to have this power, it is hoped that they will be able to develop more flexibility and speed in coping with changes in international markets.

The Russians also have need for improved coordination in dealing with their East European allies. To some extent, this is something of a surprise. When the Russians announced the formation of COMECON in January, 1949, everyone feared that a new economic monolith had been created that would outclass all competition. Officially it was claimed that COMECON would promote economic inter-relationships among the communist states of Eastern Europe by facilitating economic integration and growth through the expansion of trade. It was hailed as something that could only be done in a communist world. And, in fact, after the long struggle to form the European Common Market, something which was completed eight years later in 1957, it looked as if the Russian claims were correct. It was unexpected, therefore, when the Common Market moved rapidly ahead while COMECON stood still.

The main difficulty with COMECON was that none of the so-called partners trusted one another and they all distrusted and feared the USSR. No country was willing to agree readily to any suggestion that looked as though it would result in a loss of sovereignty, especially to the Soviet Union. Much of the fear stemmed from the rather heavy-handed methods the Russians used with their Joint Stock Companies and their pricing policies.

How badly COMECON failed can be judged by the fact that, after almost 20 years of existence, there is an insignificant amount of multilateral trade between the members of the bloc. Virtually all trade is conducted on a bilateral basis. Those countries that find themselves with an extra supply of another country's currency discover that there is usually nothing they can buy with their money. Any goods of value that have not already been committed to some bilateral trade deal are set aside for export to hard-currency countries in the West. Given the "planned nature" of the East European countries, there is usually little left over that is of any value to any other country. Since East

153

European currencies are not convertible, there is not much that can be done with any surplus accumulated by another country. To overcome such problems, the Russians have sponsored the creation of COMECON's own bank, the International Bank for Economic Cooperation. However, IBEC's success has not been much greater than COMECON's. The Poles have even complained openly that the currency of the bank must be made convertible before there can be any meaningful multilateral trade.

If COMECON has been unsuccessful in promoting multilateral trade, recently it has been able to stimulate the formation of some joint projects. In 1964, the Druzba Oil Pipeline was opened. It runs through most of East Europe and provides an outlet for Soviet oil. Similarly, the Russians have promoted the creation of an electric power grid and a joint pool of railroad cars. Also some factories have been formed which combine the resources of two or more members of the bloc. However, with vivid memories of the Soviet Joint Stock Companies still fresh in their minds, there has been considerable hesitancy about too much multilateral cooperation.

Another area where some, but only some, progress has been made is in the field of export and import pricing. As part of the reform movement which has affected almost all of the Communist countries of Eastern Europe except Rumania, new prices are being introduced. As we saw, if the price reforms which have been carried out in the USSR are any indication, some of these changes will be substantial. To some extent these changes are being made to bring domestic prices more in line with world prices. Heretofore, prices used in intrabloc trade have been patterned after world prices. Consequently the more domestic prices vary from the world price level, the more complications there are in working out an agreement and in determining what should be imported and what should be exported. More and more studies are being conducted which show that, because of poor pricing practices, the Russians should have been importing what they exported and exporting what they imported. There would be less chance of such mistakes and it would simplify matters if there was less disparity between domestic and world prices. Of course, world prices are continually fluctuating, whereas the domestic prices within the bloc tend to remain fixed for a long period of time. Conceivably there would be another problem in the unlikely event that all the countries of the world became communist. What would COMECON use for world prices then? Reportedly, when asked this question, a Polish official replied that they would always keep one country noncommunist so COMECON would have someplace to turn to find world prices that would be economically sound and superior to prices within the bloc.

REALITY: *Soviet foreign trade operations are far from being vastly more efficient than those in a noncommunist country. Regardless of the advantages which are supposed to follow from the monopoly control of foreign trade, the Soviets find themselves outmaneuvered by private traders as often as they in turn outmaneuver. Economic activity in Eastern Europe has by no means realized the potentialities that were once contemplated. At the same time, the Russians have made significant trading inroads into Western Europe. But, in almost all cases, the trade possibilities from the point of view of the noncommunist country have proven to be less than anticipated.*

CHAPTER 13

MYTH: *The Soviet Union has been a true friend and supporter of the less-developed countries of the world. In both trade and aid, the Russians have neither tied strings nor taken advantage of poorer countries.*

The reputation of the Russians in the Afro-Asian bloc is much better than they deserve. Some of the good deeds performed by the Russians in their initial contact with the countries of the developing world created a favorable image which has glorified the Russians ever since. They retain this glowing reputation despite the fact that their subsequent performance has not always measured up to their first efforts. In contrast, partly because of serious blunders in the beginning, the image of the Western countries has been very unfavorable despite the fact that there has been a significant improvement in the aid efforts of the United States and other European countries.

Actually, until Stalin's death and the end of the Korean War, the Russians cared little about the underdeveloped regions. The Russians had plenty of other problems to keep them busy. Whatever interest they had in the underdeveloped areas was primarily because of their need for various raw materials. Thus, in 1950, the Russians exported only $32 million worth of goods to these areas, while importing $93 million. Eventually, Stalin's successors came to realize the potential, both political and economic, in this area and proceeded to take advantage of it.

The Russians had much in their favor when, in 1954, they first decided to court the countries of Africa, Asia, and Latin America. The predatory performance of the Russians in the areas bordering the USSR was not well publicized in the outside world. Moreover, the Russians had virtually no economic contact or involvement with the former colonies of the West. There had of course been local Communist Parties in these areas, but the Russians were often able to disassociate themselves from local action. Consequently, the Russians had no vested interests to maintain and were free to criticize so much of what needed criticism. In contrast, most of the Western nations did have colonial interests of some sort that they sought to maintain until they found themselves forced out one way or another. For many of the discontented in the colonial areas, it often became a choice of the devil they knew and had fought or the devil they did not know and with whom they had no contact. Because the Russians entered with banners proclaiming a new order and promising support against the imperialists, the Russians generally received a warm welcome.

Beginning in 1954 when they made their first postwar loan to a neutralist country, the Russians recognized the close tie between trade and aid. Invariably the Russians found that the only way they could improve their trade balance in the Afro-Asian bloc was to offer promises of long-term credit. Over the years, the native technicians in the former colonial areas had developed a strong preference for Western goods and quality. Much as they grew to resent the English, French, and Americans, they still preferred products made in London, Paris, and Chicago. Unfortunately their desires were generally not supported by their ability to pay. These countries invariably found themselves with troublesome balances of trade and payments, especially in their dealings with the West. Taking advantage of this situation, the Russians and their allies in Eastern Europe realized that one way to sell their goods was to offer generous credits. Many officials in the developing countries eventually concluded that no matter how superior in quality and performance an American bulldozer might be to a Russian bulldozer, if there was no way to obtain the American product, then the only thing to do was to accept the Russian offer with credits.

Russian credits of course were not always tied directly to the export of a specific good (credits were also used to finance construction

157

projects and the use of specialists), but the desire to increase exports was an important element in the Russian decision to move in this direction. By increasing Soviet exports to these areas, the Soviet balance of trade with the developing nations improved rapidly. By 1955, exports had increased from the $32 million in 1950 to $142 million. Thus, exports to the developing countries almost equalled Soviet imports which had risen from $93 million to $160 million. This trend continued, and, shortly thereafter, the balance of trade swung the other way. With the exception of 1960, the Russian balance of trade with the developing countries has been in Russia's favor since at least 1958. In 1965, the Russians exported $1.2 billion of goods to this area of the world but imported only $815 million. Most of the improvement from the Soviet point of view can be directly attributed to foreign aid. The credits provided by the Russians under their aid agreements were virtually all in Russian rubles. In other words, Russian aid is predicated on the purchase of goods from the USSR. Tied aid of this sort always leads to an increase in exports even if the importer would prefer to use his credits for purchases elsewhere. The over-all effect of their aid and their growing trade surplus with the developing countries is that the Russians have acquired a trade posture which, to the developing countries, is not much different from that of the other Western countries.

To counter such criticisms of their trade policies, the Russians have declared their special concern for the needs of the developing countries. After the meeting of UNCTAD (the United Nations Conference for Trade and Development) in Geneva, in 1964, the Russians announced that they were unilaterally abolishing their tariffs on all imports from the developing countries. This announcement was greeted with something less than an emotional outpouring because most of the trade officials in these areas realized that it does not matter much what tariffs are in the USSR since the state still exercises a monopoly on all foreign trade. Thus all imports are purchased by government enterprises and tariffs are after all collected by another state enterprise so that the payment of tariffs is a bookkeeping operation and not a meaningful obstacle. The decision to import is not made by a private importer, as it is in the West, who must then determine whether or not the tariff he pays to his government makes the price of the import worthwhile.

As part of their trade and aid policy, the Russians have also relied heavily on the use of barter as a means of easing the payment problems of their partners. In such an arrangement, the Russians accept payment for their imports and their aid with the recipient country's currency. These soft currency repayments, however, are not always as attractive to the recipient as it first appears. Like the Latin Americans who found themselves enmeshed in the economic clutches of Nazi Germany, the Afro-Asian countries find that their international balance of payments position often becomes even more serious once they engage in this kind of barter. After they agree with the Russians to repay their obligations with bartered goods, they find that the Russians select the best goods produced within the country. Inevitably this means that the developing country has less to sell to the hard currency countries of the Western world. Since they have less to sell, they have even less money to buy. Consequently without offsetting loans from the West, Russia's trading partners find they must rely more and more on the Russians. In the long run this can lead to ever-increasing problems. Because Russian equipment is poorer in quality, it often turns out that in dollars expended per unit of performance (i.e., tons of dirt moved in a day), the Russian equipment is often more expensive. Thus, what looks so attractive frequently turns out to be very unsatisfactory.

Despite appearances to the contrary, there is also evidence to indicate that the Russians cannot be relied on to provide support for commodity prices like cotton, rice, cocoa, and sugar. We saw earlier how the Russians used to step in dramatically to help a particular country at a given time. But apparently, this is not a consistent policy. After the initial rescue effort, the Russians often direct their attention elsewhere. Consequently, there is often little to back up Soviet boasts that dealing with the USSR will ensure a guaranteed price and quantity of sales. Egon Neuberger, of Stony Brook University, and Frederic Pryor, of Swarthmore College, have both found that Soviet trade commitments are at best equal to but generally less favorable than similar transactions in Western Europe, the United States, and Japan.[1]

---

[1] "Is the USSR Superior to the West as a Market for Primary Products?" *Review of Economics and Statistics,* Aug., 1964, p. 287; also, "Trade Barriers of Capitalist and Communist Nations Against Foodstuffs Exported by Tropical Underdeveloped Nations," *ibid.,* Nov., 1966, p. 406.

Although the desire to improve their balance of payments was one important reason for Soviet foreign aid, there have been other considerations which were of equal or more importance. First, there were some Russians who sincerely felt that their government has a responsibility to help less fortunate countries. These people are sometimes able to translate their feelings into concrete government action. But second and probably most important in determining the nature of Soviet foreign aid is the political self-interest of the Soviet Union. Because they were on the outside looking into these areas prior to 1954, foreign aid has been a convenient device for extending the Soviet sphere of influence. The promise of economic and often military help made it possible for the Russians to establish a political presence in many areas which previous Russian governments never dreamed of influencing.

Many recipients welcomed Soviet help not only because of the promise of increased economic development but because the possibility of Soviet involvement in the area was a valuable counter in negotiations with the traditional colonial powers. Sometimes this caused the Western countries to increase their bids of foreign aid, and sometimes it made it possible for countries like Cuba to run the risk of economic boycott by the United States. It seems fair to say that Soviet foreign aid provided the economic backing which helped make possible a political policy of neutralism. Without the alternative economic aid offered by the USSR, few countries would have risked such an independent stature.

In evaluating Soviet foreign aid, it can be said that the Russians seem to have obtained a higher return for their money than we have in terms of economic development and political appreciation. Between 1954 and mid-1967, the Russians committed themselves to slightly less than $4 billion worth of economic aid to neutralist areas. Of this, no more than 40 per cent, or about $1.6 billion, has actually been delivered. In contrast the United States had authorized and spent about $52 billion, or about 13 times as much, since 1949. It is hard to draw up precise statistics to measure exactly how much more productive Soviet aid has been compared with American aid because it is hard to place a value on such seemingly nonproductive acts as the shipment of American wheat to India. Thus the United States has spent over $6 billion in India of which $3 billion was for food, compared with approximately $1 billion of commitments from the Soviet Union, most of which was intended for industrial purposes. Millions of lives were saved by the American wheat, but what is the economic and political value of such aid? Some Indians even argue that it would have been heartless, but it might have been better for India if the American wheat had not been supplied. Then India would have been shocked into a more serious recognition of its population and agricultural problem and would have taken steps sooner to contend with it. As it was, American wheat kept the price of local wheat down, which dampened a needed stimulus for the native farmers. By making it possible for India to avoid facing up to its birth control needs, American wheat may also have made possible a population larger than is economically justified in India. In any case, most Indians seem to feel that, even if American food aid is excluded, on a dollar per dollar basis, Soviet aid has had the greater impact. Some even feel that the smaller total expenditure of Soviet aid has been more effective than the total expenditure of American aid.

The reason Soviet aid has made such an impact is that the Russians tend to concentrate their efforts on industrial projects such as the Aswan Dam in the United Arab Republic and the Bhilai and Bokaro Steel Mills in India. The recipients of such aid view these projects as a direct benefit to their efforts at industrialization. Naturally this pleases them. Soviet efforts, however, have not always turned out to be as successful as they have been in India. In Indonesia, Ghana, and Kenya, for example, Soviet efforts have not only failed economically, they have also failed politically, especially in Indonesia and Ghana. In such countries, the Russian projects have been built without regard to the proper scale of operations in the country. Moreover, the Russians have been as eager as the United States to sell military equipment to such countries. As in the United States, this is done to gain or maintain a political foothold and to provide an outlet for excess munition stocks. Like the United States, the USSR has a gigantic munitions industry, which it must sustain and finance. Sales of this equipment on credit to developing countries has made the USSR one of the world's largest arms merchants, second only to the United States. However, as the Russians themselves have noted by this time, the sale of a billion dollars' worth of equipment to both

161

the United Arab Republic and Indonesia has not always produced results which have been favorable to the long-run interests of the USSR. Like their tendency to build factories without careful regard to size and efficiency, the sale of munitions by the Russians often leads to repayment problems. Such projects do not provide for the generation of large enough sums of foreign exchange or exportable commodities. This has actually led to repayment defaults by several of the countries. In addition, some countries have discovered that there are strings tied to Soviet aid. When it looks as though the borrowers will not be able to repay their loans, the Russians, like any lender, tend to take steps to ensure that the loans will be repaid. They halt deliveries of their goods and leave construction projects unfinished. The Russians protested loudly when their sympathizers were deposed in Ghana and Indonesia. They were even more outspoken at the anti-Soviet policies of China, Albania, and, at one time, Yugoslavia.

Over the years the Russians have found that they, too, have developed vested interests in many areas outside of their borders. Initially, they found themselves occupied only in Eastern Europe and then China. Today, unlike the pre-1954 period, the Russians find that they are affected by what happens in Ghana, Indonesia, Pakistan, India, and the Middle East and even Cuba. No longer can the Russians roam about like an irritating gadfly oblivious to the consequences. Like the United States, the Russians find that unrest or political change in these areas can be harmful to their economic and political policies. There are still many areas where the Soviets can inflict damage on American interests, but now there are similar opportunities for the Americans to disturb Russian interests. The only ones with little or nothing to lose today are the Chinese.

As Russia has moved into international economic affairs as an involved participant, it has begun to take a new look at some issues. Russia's new vested interest in international affairs may help to account for Russia's role in bringing about a peaceful settlement between India and Pakistan. It may also account for Russia's relative restraint in Egypt. Although the Russians were quite inflammatory in their speeches about Israel, their actions, once the conflict began, were quite conservative, at times embarrassingly so.

As Russia finds itself more and more involved in international activities, the character of its activities takes on an increasingly traditional pattern. For instance, as they find themselves running short of some natural resources, they have begun to call openly for greater reliance on foreign raw materials.[2] The ramifications of this change in policy are intriguing. On the one hand, as we have noted, the Russians say that one of the main reasons for the exhaustion of their raw material base is that they have been selling these raw materials to the communist countries of Eastern Europe at unrealistically low prices. This is largely because of their past failure to include rent and interest as a cost. On the other hand, this has led several economists to urge that Soviet foreign aid be directed to those developing countries where its use will help to generate the reverse flow of raw materials to the USSR. They talk of their need for tin, copper, zinc, aluminum, rubber, iron ore, gas, and even cotton and oil. This is exactly what the Russians have accused the United States of doing in the past, only then the Russians called it exploitation.

Reflecting this new outlook on international life, the Russians have even started to make direct investments overseas. They have joined with local citizens to form joint stock companies for the sale and service of automobiles in Finland, for the operation of a department store and possibly an oil refinery in Belgium, and for the conduct of an international trade firm in Morocco and Nigeria. While the size of the investment thus far is still very modest, the Russians no doubt find themselves reflecting on the recent advice of a Yugoslav government official. He, too, advocated direct investment overseas as a method of reducing balance-of-payment difficulties. With some indignation, however, he cautioned that Yugoslav officials should take care to see that the country they invest in does not follow a policy of nationalization! Communism has come a long way from the dreams of the Revolution.

REALITY: *The Russians have played an important role in stimulating the economic growth of underdeveloped countries. At times Soviet trade and aid have proved to be of vital impor-*

[2] *Voprosy Ekonomiki*, Feb., 1965, p. 78; Apr., 1966, p. 85; and May, 1966, p. 83.

tance and quite successful. At other times, however, Russian aid and trade have been a failure. There have even been times when Russian aid has benefited the USSR more than the recipient country. As the USSR finds itself drawn more and more into the world stream of commerce and development, it finds itself developing vested interests in areas remote from the Soviet Union. This has led to economic attitudes and activities which seem little if at all different from those of other developed countries.

CONCLUSION

By now our study of the myths and realities in the Soviet economy should have indicated just how complex the Soviet society is. There is a little something for everyone. By approaching the problem this way, we may have been able to make the point that life in the USSR is not just a matter of blacks and whites; sometimes it does not even appear to be gray.

In a real sense, the Soviet system is a dual society. To economists, this means that the modern and productive sector of the economy exists side by side with the primitive and backward sector. Gradually, the modern sector is gaining. At the same time, the dual society also seems an appropriate way to describe the Soviet political conditions that affect economic life. There are free conditions and unfree conditions. Hopefully, here, too, the modern sector—that is, the free political conditions—will grow.

Much of what seems to be happening now as well as what will happen in the future is probably linked with the success the Russians have had in implementing their economic reforms. It is unlikely that the Russians will ever permit the existence of private enterprise in anything other than small and limited forms of economic activity. But in their drive to develop a more perfect form of state capitalism, they may find themselves reducing the arbitrary role of the state. As the economy expands and becomes more complex, it becomes harder to control centrally. Even with the use of improved computers and communication, arbitrary use of power tends to cause disruption. As the British economist Peter Wiles put it, Lenin may have been right when he insisted that only centralized power could make the trains run on time—but Lenin never had to face the task of guiding a million automobiles. In the same way as the society becomes more complex, there are similar problems of guidance which are not easily mastered through unified control.

The problem is much the same in the international sphere. With the growing rush of technology comes a need for more interchange of materials and knowledge. Thus, if they want to compete, the Russians find it necessary to become more involved with the world. Only in this way can they share in the improvements in technology and production that are taking place at such a rapid rate.

Increasingly, the Russians find themselves facing the same problems as the other advanced countries of the world. Not surprisingly, therefore, the Russians find that they are responding in the same way. This does not mean convergence, nor does it necessarily mean peace. After all, Hitler ran a very advanced country and still fought a war. But it may provide a better base for understanding, and in this there may be hope. Perhaps it is not too much of a myth to believe that, in better understanding of economic reality on both sides, there may be room for improved harmony.

SELECTED BIBLIOGRAPHY

American Iron and Steel Institute, *Steel in the Soviet Union* (New York, 1959).

Ames, Edward, *Soviet Economic Processes* (Homewood, Ill., 1965).

Baykov, Alexander, *The Development of the Soviet Economic System* (Cambridge, England, 1948).

────── *Soviet Foreign Trade* (Princeton, 1946).

Bergson, Abram, *The Economics of Soviet Planning* (New Haven, 1964).

────── and S. Kuznets, *Economic Trends in the Soviet Union* (Cambridge, Mass., 1963).

────── *The Real National Income of Soviet Russia Since 1928* (Cambridge, Mass., 1961).

────── (ed.), *Soviet Economic Growth* (New York, 1953).

────── *Structure of Soviet Wages* (Cambridge, Mass., 1944).

Berliner, Joseph, *Factory and Manager in the U.S.S.R.* (Cambridge, Mass., 1957).

────── *Soviet Economic Aid* (New York, 1958).

Bornstein, Morris and Daniel Fusfeld (eds.), *The Soviet Economy: A Book of Readings* (Homewood, Ill., 1966).

Brown, Emily Clark, *Soviet Trade Unions and Labor Relations* (Cambridge, Mass., 1966).

Campbell, Robert, *Accounting in Soviet Planning and Management* (Cambridge, Mass., 1963).

────── *Soviet Economic Power: Its Organization, Growth and Challenge* (Boston, 1966).

Chapman, Janet, *Real Wages in Soviet Russia Since 1928* (Cambridge, Mass., 1963).

Clark, M. Gardner, *The Economics of Soviet Steel* (Cambridge, Mass., 1956).

Cohn, Stanley, "Soviet Growth Retardation: Trends in Resource Availability and Efficiency," *New Directions in the Soviet Economy,* Joint Economic Committee (Washington, D.C., 1966).

Degras, Jane (ed.), *Soviet Planning Essays in Honor of Naum Jasny* (New York, 1964).

Deutscher, I., *Soviet Trade Unions* (New York, 1950).

Dewar, M., *Soviet Trade with Eastern Europe* (New York, 1951).

Dewitt, Nicholas, *Education and Professional Employment in the USSR* (Washington, D.C., 1961).

—————— *Soviet Professional Manpower: Its Education, Training and Supply* (Washington, D.C., 1954).

Dobb, Maurice, *Soviet Economic Development Since 1917* (London, 1966).

Domar, Evsey, *Essays on the Theory of Economic Growth* (Oxford, 1957).

Erlich, A., *The Soviet Industrialization Debate* (Cambridge, Mass., 1960).

Felker, Jere, *Soviet Economic Controversies* (Cambridge, Mass., 1966).

Gerschenkron, A., *Economic Backwardness in Historical Perspective* (Cambridge, Mass., 1963).

Goldman, Marshall I., *Comparative Economic Systems: A Reader* (New York, 1963).

—————— *Soviet Foreign Aid* (New York, 1967).

—————— *Soviet Marketing: Distribution in a Controlled Economy* (New York, 1963).

Granick, David, *Management in the Industrial Firm in the U.S.S.R.* (New York, 1954).

—————— *The Red Executive* (New York, 1960).

—————— *Soviet Metal-Fabricating and Economic Development* (Madison, Wisconsin, 1967).

Grossman, Gregory, *Soviet Statistics of Physical Output of Industrial Commodities* (Princeton, 1960).

───── (ed.), *Value and Plan* (Berkeley, 1960).

Holzman, Franklyn D. (ed.), *Readings on the Soviet Economy* (Chicago, 1962).

───── *Soviet Taxation* (Cambridge, Mass., 1955).

Hunter, Holland, *Soviet Transportation Policy* (Cambridge, Mass., 1957).

Jasny, Naum, *Essays on the Soviet Economy* (New York, 1962).

───── *Soviet Industrialization, 1928-1952* (Chicago, 1961).

Joint Economic Committee, Congress of the United States, *Comparisons of the United States and Soviet Economies* (Washington, D.C., 1959), 3 vols.

───── *New Directions in the Soviet Economy* (Washington, D.C., 1966).

Karcz, Jerzy, "Thoughts on the Grain Problem," *Soviet Studies,* April 1967, p. 339.

Kaser, Michael, *Comecon, Integration Problems of the Planned Economies* (Oxford, 1965).

Kovner, M., *The Challenge of Coexistence: A Study of Soviet Economic Diplomacy* (Washington, D.C., 1961).

Leeman, Wayne A., *Capitalism, Market Socialism, and Central Planning: Readings in Comparative Economic Systems* (Boston, Mass., 1963).

Lenin, V. I., *The Development of Capitalism in Russia. Selected Works,* vol. I (London, 1936).

Levine, Herbert, "The Centralized Planning of Supply in Soviet Industry," *Comparison of the United States and Soviet Economies* (Washington, D.C.: U.S. Congress, Joint Economic Committee, 1959), p. 151.

Lyashchenko, Peter I., *History of the National Economy to the 1917 Revolution,* tr. L. M. Herman (New York, 1949).

Montias, J. M., "Planning with Material Balances," *American Economic Review,* December 1959, p. 963.

Moorsteen, Richard, and Raymond Powell, *The Soviet Capital Stock, 1928-1962* (Homewood, Ill., 1966).

Neuberger, Egon, "The Yugoslav Investment Auctions," *Quarterly Journal of Economics,* February 1959, p. 88.

Nove, Alec, *The Soviet Economy: An Introduction* (New York, 1965).

———— and D. Donnelly, *Trade with Communist Countries* (London, 1960).

Nutter, Warren, *The Growth of Industrial Production in the Soviet Union* (Princeton, 1962).

Oxenfeldt, A. R., *Economic Systems in Action* (New York, 1958).

Pryor, Frederic, *The Communist Foreign Trade System* (Cambridge, Mass., 1963).

Richman, Barry, *Soviet Management* (Englewood Cliffs, New Jersey, 1965).

Schwartz, Harry, *Russia's Soviet Economy,* 2nd ed. (Englewood Cliffs, N.J., 1958).

Shaffer, Harry, *The Soviet Economy* (New York, 1963).

Smolinski, Leon, "Planning Without Theory 1917-67," *Survey,* July, 1967, p. 108.

Spulber, Nicolas, *The Soviet Economy: Structure, Principles, Problems* (New York, 1962).

———— *Soviet Strategy for Economic Growth* (Bloomington, Indiana, 1964).

Ward, Benjamin, *The Socialist Economy* (New York, 1967).

Wellisz, Stanislaw, *The Economies of the Soviet Bloc* (New York, 1964).

Wilcox, C., W. D. Weatherford, Jr., and H. Hunter, *Economies of the World Today: Their Organization, Development, and Performance* (New York, 1962).

Wiles, P. J. D., *The Political Economy of Communism* (Cambridge, Mass., 1962).

Williams, Ernest W., *Freight Transportation in the Soviet Union: A Comparison with the United States* (New York, 1959).

Zauberman, Alfred, *Economic Imperialism: The Lesson of Eastern Europe* (London, 1955).

A

Abramov, Fyodr, 47
Afghanistan, 61, 145
Africa, 18
Aganbegian, A. G., 5
Agriculture, 10, 11, 21, 24, 63
  collectivization of, 26-27, 31,
    33-34, 64-67, 100
  inefficiency in, 99-103
Albania, 162
All Union Committee for Material and Technical Supply,
  128
American Iron and Steel Institute, 81
Antonov, O. K., 120
Aswan Dam, 161

B

Baby boom, 50
Ballod, Karl, 28-29
Belgium, 163
Bergson, Abram, 34
Berliner, Joseph, 72
Berman, A., 129
Blue Cross, 44
Bolshevichka, 125

Bolshevik Revolution, 12, 14-18,
  27, 30, 32
Bonus, 90-91, 124, 127
Bornstein, Morris, 99
Brezhnev, 102
Bulgaria, 148
Bureaucracy (See Government:
  bureaucracy)

C

Campbell, Robert, 89, 119
Capital, 5, 31, 96, 127
  decentralization of, 130
  output ratios, 23, 87
Capitalism, 17, 19, 22, 111-12
  in USSR, 137-41
Changchun Railroad (Chinese
  Eastern Railroad), 146, 148
China, 9, 12, 18, 138-39, 146,
  148-49, 162
City planning, 107-8
Cohn, Stanley, 34, 63
Collective Farms (*see* Kolkhozy)
Collectivization (*see* Agriculture:
  collectivization of)
COMECON, 146, 153-55
Communications, 118

Communist Party, 14, 16-17, 71-73
Consumer goods, 23, 33, 53-58, 63, 95, 97, 113, 121-23
  automobiles, 57, 138-39
Consumption, 120-23, 129, 133
  see also Economic planning; Standard of living
Cooperative stores, 66
Council for Mutual Economic Assistance (*see* COMECON)
Credit, 115-16
  foreign, 157-58
  installmental, 134
Critique of the Gotha Program, 19
Cuba, 160, 162
Czarist government, 12-13, 41, 61
Czechoslovakia, 63, 138, 148, 153

D

Day in the New Life, 47
Denmark, 112
DeWitt, Nicholas, 43
Dissent (See Government: totalitarian nature of)
Dostoevsky, 12
Druzba Oil Pipeline, 154
"Dual economy," 9-10, 165
Dudintsev, V., 88
Dymshits, V., 120, 128

E

Economic development, 79-85, 87-89

Economic development (*Cont.*)
  and collectivization, 27-29
  before 1914, 9-13, 15, 23, 31
  decline of, 119
  via Five Year Plans, 28
  measurement of, 3-5, 34
  under alternate economic form, 30-36, 79
Economic planning
  under NEP, 22-24
  problems of, 120-23
  reforms in, 49-50, 124-36
  theory of, 112-17
  War Communism, 1917-1921, 21
  1914-1917, 20-21
  1928-present, 28-29, 81-84, 87-99
Education, 11-12, 42-44, 59-60, 61, 63, 71
Egypt, 9, 31, 161-62
England, 9, 15, 17, 112, 145, 146, 151
European Common Market, 153

F

Fiat, 57
Field, Mark, 45
Finland, 146, 163
Five Year Plans, 28-29, 31-32, 90
  1966-1970 plan, 97, 129
Foreign relations, 145-64
Foreign trade, 158
  imports, 58, 97, 152
France, 9, 10, 15, 17, 31, 57, 145, 151

G

Gagarin, Yuri, 80
Galbraith, John Kenneth, 139
Georges Banks, 82
Germany, 9, 10, 12, 14, 15, 17, 32, 35, 63, 147-48, 152
Gerschenkron, Alexander, 10, 31
Ghana, 161-62
GOELRO (State Commission for Electrification), 28
Gogol, 12
Gosbank, 115, 127, 128
Gosplan (State Planning Commission), 28, 93, 113-14
Government
  bureaucracy, 75-76, 86-87
  favoritism in, 72-73
  totalitarian nature of, 39-41, 62, 67-69, 71-73
Grossman, Gregory, 99

H

Holzman, Franklyn D., 65
Housing, 33, 52-53, 63, 74, 82-83
Hungary, 16, 138, 148-49, 153
Hunter, Holland, 119
Hydroelectric construction, 96

I

Iagodkin, 50
Iamarka (trade fair), 129
Incentives, 11, 24, 90, 96, 102, 114
India, 9, 12, 160-61
Indonesia, 161-62

Industrialization, 4, 9, 10, 21, 31, 61, 63, 80-83
  see also Economic development
Internal Passport, 41
International Bank for Economic Cooperation (IBEC), 154
International Conference on Techniques of Demand Analysis, 134
Intourist, 117
Inventories, 118-20
Investment, 63, 113
  agricultural, 100
  and Development Fund, 129-30
  and forced savings, 83-84
Ireland, 18
Israel, 36, 162
Italy, 9, 18, 35, 57

J

Japan, 9, 32, 35-36, 97, 112, 146, 159
John Birch Society, 114
Johnson, Lyndon, 40
Joint Stock Companies, 146-49, 153-54

K

Kantorovich, L. V., 119
Karcz, Jerzy F., 25, 33
Kazakhstan, 100
Kenya, 161
Khrushchev, 31, 52, 65, 82, 95, 100, 102, 125
Kislovodsk, 105-6

Kolkhozy (collective farms) (*see* Agriculture), 26, 27, 64-66, 103
Kosygin, Alexei, 43, 51, 97, 102, 125-28, 139, 140
Kronstadt Naval Base, 21-22

L

Labor, 41-43, 47, 49-50, 60
Labor Books, 42
Labor Reserve Schools, 42
Lake Baikal, 104
Latin America, 14, 18
Lenin, 14, 16-17, 21-23, 28, 31, 44, 111-12, 145, 165
Leningrad, 16, 21, 80
Levine, Herbert, 93
Liberman, Evsei, 119, 124-26, 141
Lobachevsky, N. I., 11
Lomanosov, M. V., 11

M

Machine Tractor Station, 64-65
Maiak, 125
Manchukuo, 146
Manevich, 50
Marketing, 151
   research in, 132-34
Marshall Plan, 63
Marx, Karl, 15, 17-19, 44, 132
Marxism
   ideological alterations in USSR, 15, 17, 21, 23, 27-29, 134-35
   principles of, 16-17
Maslova, 50

Medical care, 44-46, 63
Medicare, 44
Mendeleev, D. I., 11
Mexico, 36
Military equipment, 161-62
Ministry of Fishing, 81
Ministry of Foreign Trade, 151-52
Ministry of Steel, 93
Minority groups, 61, 73-74
Mongolia, 146-47
Morocco, 163
Moscow, 74, 80, 97, 117
Moussorgsky, 12

N

Nationalization, 20-21, 26-27, 29, 33, 83
Nemchinov, V. S., 119
"Nepmen," 22
Nepotism, 73
   see also Government: Favoritism in
Netherlands, 15, 17, 63
Neuberger, Egon, 159
New Economic Policy (NEP), 22-24, 28
New Zealand, 112
Nigeria, 163
Not By Bread Alone, 88
Nove, Alec, 90

P

Paris Commune, 14
Pavlov, I. P., 11
Peasantry
   conditions of, 10-11, 47, 51, 64-67

Peasantry (*Cont.*)
conservatism of, 16, 20, 27
economic role of, 20-22, 24-27, 71, 102
as revolutionary base, 16, 18
Pensions, 46-47, 64, 102
"Piggyback" concept, 87
Poland, 16, 49, 63, 138, 147, 149, 153
Police, 41
Pollution, 103-7
Port Arthur, 148
Prices, 4-5, 98, 113-14
agricultural, 64-65
imports and exports, 154-55
and NEP, 22, 24
reforms in, 131-32
retail, 66
satellite discrimination in, 148-49
Private Plots, 64-66, 102
Productivity, 5, 24, 34, 81, 93
agricultural, 99-100 (see also agriculture)
and employment, 49-50
and innovation, 94
and pollution, 106
Profits, 11, 90, 98, 112, 124, 127
agricultural, 26
Proletariat, 16-18, 20, 24
and the Party, 71
Pryor, Frederic, 159
Pushkin, 12

Q

Quality, 118, 126, 151, 159 (see also consumer goods)
and targets, 92-93

R

Reform, economic, 49-50, 124-41, 165
Renault, 57
Rent, 127
Resources
land usage, 107-8
pollution of, 103-7
Rumania, 148, 154
Russification, 74 (*see also* Minority groups)

S

Science, 11-12
atomic energy, 80, 89
space, 79-80, 89
"Scissors crisis," 24
"Second Russian Revolution," 27
Siberia, 47, 107
Smolinski, Leon, 28, 87
Social mobility, 72-73
Social Security, 46-50, 63
Solzhenitsyn, Alexander, 49, 68
Sovkhoz (state farms), 103
Stalin, 1-2, 23-28, 31, 33, 40-42, 51-52, 58, 65, 69, 74, 84, 96, 100, 112, 114, 124, 148
Stalin, Vasily, 72
Standard of living, 50-58, 60
before 1950's, 63
Statistics
availability of, 1-3
problems with, 3-5, 9, 32
Stalin's misuse of, 25-26
Steel production, 95, 99
Stolypin Reforms, 11, 16
"Storming," 92
St. Petersburg, 16

Strikes, 70
Sweden, 32
Switzerland, 81

T

Taiwan, 36
Targets, 119, 124 (*see also* Quality)
Tashkent, 61, 74
Tax, 65, 68, 98-99, 114
Tchaikovsky, 11
Technology, 79-81, 89, 93-94
    research in, 94
Toda, Yashusi, 36
Tolstoy, 12
Trade unions, 69-71, 75
Trans-Siberian Railroad, 10-11
Trapeznikov, V. A., 119
Travel, 58-59, 117
Tse-tung, Mao, 18
Tscolkovsky, K. E., 11
Turkey, 145

U

Unemployment, 47-50
    compensation, lack of, 46-50

United Nations Conference for Trade and Development (UNCTAD), 158
United States, 4, 9, 32, 34-35, 43-46, 51, 55-57, 63, 67, 80, 82, 83, 87, 101, 104-5, 112, 115, 119, 128, 146, 150, 159, 160-61, 163
Uzbekistan, 61

V

Val system, 90-92

W

Wages, 46, 51, 64, 70, 90, 114
War Communism, 21, 24
Wiles, Peter, 96, 165
Women, 60
World War II
    effect on economic development, 34
    effect on social mobility, 72

Y

Yugoslavia, 36, 49, 138, 147-48, 162

MA

N